Yes! Blessings,

SAY "YES!" TO LIFE

Judy Pearson

Ki Communication Programs ❖ Portland, Oregon

In case studies throughout this book, the names of individuals have been changed to protect personal identity. Although the author followed a course of cancer treatment that did not include chemotherapy, the purpose of this book, as it applies to health issues, is not to renounce the advice of physicians and other health care professionals, but to supplement medical treatment with the course of action suggested here.

Cover and Text Design: Heather Kibbey, www.npcbooks.com

Cover Photo: John Foxx, Getty Images, www.getty images.com

"Antidote" Photos: F. Byron Kibbey, npcbooks.com

Copyright © 2008 by Judy Pearson

Printed in the United States of America.

ISBN 13: 978-0-9816415-0-8
ISBN 10: 0-9816415-0-4

Published by:

Ki Communications
515 NW Saltzman Rd. #749
Portland, OR, 97229
Phone: 503-520-0105

Email: JudySpeak@aol.com
Author's Website: www.JudyPearson.com

Dedication

To all the Auntie Mames in life—the people who spark our curiosity and inspire us to be more than we believe we can be—I thank you for recognizing and honoring the unconquerable Spirit within all and the divine commitment to making a difference in the world. Thank you for being You.

❀ ❀ ❀

Acknowledgments

"So what are you writing about?" Every time someone asked me that, I felt like the character in the movie "*Sideways,*" who had a new and different answer every time. I admit that this book has undergone more metamorphoses than a butterfly, until it has finally reached a wonderful final stage.

As always, I've followed and greatly appreciated the teachings of: Ernest Holmes, founder of the Religious Science movement; American author and orator, Ralph Waldo Emerson; Ilchi Lee, author of *Human Technology*; Aikido Training, Portland; Guru Sai Maa Lakshmi Devi and the practice of Sukyo Mahikari, where I continue to learn various life skills that I share in this book.

I would like to thank the many friends and family members who supported me when I was searching for the right path for my message to take. Very special thanks to Heather Kibbey of NW Publishers Consortium, for her loving, patient editing and suggestions. To Annette Meredith and Diane Gronholm, for careful proofreading. To Mary Midkiff, for her unwavering support: none of her friends are dumb. To Mary Reynolds, who wouldn't take "No" for an answer. To my loving family: daughter Susan, son Ron, my grandson Ian, my granddaughters, Wensdai, Naomi, and Ivory and my sweet Aunt Daisy White.

Readers have praised—

Say "Yes!" to Life

"Judy captures the truth that to say 'Yes!' to one's life is to honor their soul."

The Reverend Jody Stevenson

"'Judy is a beautiful example of living life in the 'Yes!' mode. She lives her life by the principles she shares with her readers.

Billie White

"As I read Judy's opening story I knew it was a ubiquitous story. We have all felt the crushing limitations that restrict and prevent living the lives we really want. Judy presents a way to activate mind, body and spirit to live, truly live, the life we really want. I said "YES!" to this uplifting book. "

Flora Novarra, MS
Communication Specialist

And the outstanding presentations of Judy Pearson—

"Your dynamic presentation with your special brand of humor inspired and motivated, I would recommend your presentation to anyone wanting an inspiring speaker on communication and change."

Legacy Healthcare System

"We always look forward to having you as part of our ongoing staff trainings. Your motivational style helps us deliver outstanding customer service."

Kirby Blankenship ,
Hallmark Inn and Resorts

Table of Contents

Say "Yes!" to Life

*I*f you want to say "Yes!" to your life and live authentically, and purposefully, this book is for you. If you long for your true self to be expressed, if you want to have the balls or guts to stand up for your life and live it authentically, powerfully and in balance, keep reading. The following chapters are designed to bring your mind, body and spirit into balance so that you can experience the life of wealth, health and abundance you so richly deserve.

This book is not just to be read. It also provides a visceral experience to assist you in acquiring a new way of living fully and as you turn the pages, you are required to be fully present, in mind, body and spirit. The unique self-paced format of this book and the various Ki exercises will encourage and inspire you to take charge of your life and realize the power of your unique presence, while opening your self up to an extraordinary life.

You may be wondering what makes me an "expert" on saying "Yes!" to life. Beyond my professional training and career as a Religious Science practitioner, a counselor, author and speaker, my "expertise" comes from various life enriching experiences and the way I approach life.

For me, life is a safari, an exploration, if you will. Around every bush, tree or rock is a challenge out of which comes a lesson.

I considered waiting until the safari was over, until I knew absolutely everything there is to know about life before I began writing this book. Of course I haven't reached that stage of perfect wisdom and I've concluded that there is no end to the exploration and expedition of life. So waiting around until you've absorbed a lifetime of knowledge before you share what you have learned is ludicrous.

The Sin of Not Sharing

It's been said that the greatest sin of all is to have the gift of knowledge and not share it with the world. Expertise comes from the exploration and utilization of life's experiences. This will be a theme we'll follow throughout this book as you learn to develop your own skill in exploring your experiences to live a joyful and enriched life.

So let me share one of my own life experiences, one that opened my eyes, mind and soul to saying "Yes!" to life.

Starting on The Path to My New Life

A century ago, or so it seems—actually 25 years ago—I was diagnosed with cancer. My doctor performed a hysterectomy and insisted I start chemotherapy treatments immediately.

Stunned, I sat there, searching for words. Finally I blurted out, "My mind… my mind doesn't believe in chemotherapy."

Without a pause he said, "Your mind has nothing to do with it. There are no other effective alternatives." Then he dismissed me with, "I know you're scared, but here are your chemotherapy papers."

At the shock of the revelation and my limited prospects, I was taken aback. My course of action was laid out in black and white. No negotiating. A doctor—who certainly knew far more than I about cancer—was telling me what was best. But still I kept thinking, "Chemotherapy is poison and poison kills." At best, chemo seemed like small bandage on an elephantine wound; at best a temporary solution.

Let me clearly state that I'm not condemning chemotherapy; I'm sure it helps thousands. I just had to do what I felt was right for me. What I haven't told you was that this was not the first, but the *second* time, I'd faced the trauma of a cancer diagnosis. At the age of nineteen, when cancer was discovered in one of my glands, I was told I had a life expectancy of just two years. By changing my environment, I had surpassed that by twenty years. So years later, when the second round hit, I had more than an inkling of how taking charge of life could change the circumstances of one's life.

Could My Mind Control My Body's Well-being?

Deep down, this thought came to me: I felt that the mind was surely powerful enough to control my body's well-being. What was I doing that was making me ill? And if so, could I change the direction of my illness? Somehow I knew that if I wanted to change my health, I had to take a closer look at the way I perceived life, or cancer was going to just keep reappearing and eating away at me until there was no more Judy. I sensed that I had strayed away from my true nature and lost my self. Nothing was going to change unless *I* changed.

I had read enough self-help books and listened to enough audio tapes to be dangerous. Nevertheless, I made a decision that went against all conventional thinking at the time: I opted *not* to take chemotherapy treatments. And like linoleum flooring in an earthquake, my life began to shift, ripple and crack, never to be the same again.

The doctor's words, although abrupt, motivated me to take action. Not knowing where to begin, I tried hundreds of remedies: diets, psychology, vitamin doses, affirmations and meditations. Even coffee enemas. (Yes, I was desperate!) I pounded the pavement, consulting naturopaths, chiropractors and health food stores. I was so unaccustomed to this lifestyle, I thought you had to wear Birkenstocks and never shave you legs to even set foot in a place like that. Oh, my God— the list went on forever. All these things played a part in my getting well and staying healthy, yet none of them were paramount factors.

I Had, Unknowingly, Said "Yes!" to Life

What I didn't realize, at the time, was that I had already done the most important thing I could do. I had said "Yes!" to Life. I had stepped up and taken charge of the vision I wanted for my life. My true self was emerging as I made decisions based on my instincts and how I wanted my life to be, not on what some else thought it should be.

"Courageous risks are life giving; they help you grow, make you brave and better than you think you are."
Joan L. Curcio

What I discovered along the way was that expressing my true self and being authentic to myself is the key to living fully. Rearranging my perspectives and priorities opened up for me a whole new world of abundance, health and happiness.

Assertiveness Is The Hub

Through my twenty years of exploration and research I grew to understand that *assertiveness is the "hub" of the wheel of life.* It is assertiveness, this saying 'Yes!" to life, that is the key to a person's entire well being. It affects every aspect of life. Your level of assertiveness determines how well you eat, how much fun you have, how well you communicate, how you develop loving relationships, and the amount of stress you have in life.

To be clear, I am not talking about fighting for life by becoming more *aggressive*. I did not fight cancer. I grew to love my cancer. There was nothing to fight *for* or *against*. Cancer, like all other life experiences, provides an opportunity to stand up, take inventory and appreciate your life.

The point is this: my perceptions of life and my preceding actions caused my cancer. I had, as a child, decided that the world was a hard place to live and the best way to survive was to avoid problems, wait until the problem disappeared and/or just stuff my feelings of anger and frustration back inside. If I blended into the corner of the room, kept my thoughts to myself and nodded my head in agreement I wouldn't have to face the consequences of ridicule or physical abuse.

As Judy says:

You don't have to experience a major health crisis or other personal calamity to wake up and truly live your life. However if that's what it takes, that's what it takes. If you or someone you know is facing one of life's challenges right now and you feel sorry, don't. Celebrate the awakening and unfolding of life.

On the surface was a calm, passive and nice Judy. On the inside was a seething, desperate woman letting things eat away at her. You see, I thought being nice and keeping the peace was the answer to all my problems. It was how I had survived as a child. However, the "nice" youngster was not serving me well in my adult years. As strange as it may seem, keeping myself peaceful, making everything "nice" was really only keeping the peace *from* me. I was sending a message to myself and others that what I thought or said didn't really matter. Needless to say, the results flushed my self-esteem down the toilet along with my confidence and health.

Once I understood the *Universal Law of Attraction*, I appreciated how cancer was inevitably in my cards. Here's how it goes:

The Universal Law of Attraction

Whatever our subconscious mind holds long enough is bound to be produced in our external affairs. Our subconscious mind is the medium in which we live and move and have our being on the subjective side of life.

But, like all card games, it's the advice of The Gambler, Kenny Rogers, that holds true, "You got to know when to hold'em and know when to fold'em." And I might add: Play the cards you are dealt to the best of your ability.

Practicing The Art of Letting Go

As I worked toward letting go of old, limiting thought patterns and the people who supported those thoughts, I rediscovered my true self, the spirit within. I gained confidence and began to communicate my true feelings, wants and needs. Some friends and family members backed away. It wasn't easy losing friends or having people look at me as though I were crazy, but I had to take the risk because my life depended upon it.

One year later, I went back to the doctor for a full examination. Looking at my chart, he went down the exhaustive list of tests. "Judy, all your tests have come back negative," he said, surprised. "There are no signs of cancer…what have you been doing?"

Like a typical new convert, I spouted my newfound 'religion': "I'm eating healthy, exercising, and studying philosophy and religions." And with hardly a breath I continued, "It seems to be working for me, don't you think?"

His reply stung. "You are doing really well, and what you have been doing is good for you but there is *no proof* that this will help you get rid of cancer." And he went on, just like a broken record, "I must still strongly recommend chemotherapy."

After several years had passed and I remained cancer-free, I had one of those moments when I knew I must share my knowledge, so I decided to write my first book, *Healthy Mind, Healthy Body: Using Your Mind Power to Stay Healthy and Overcome Illness*. Soon I was invited to speak and give workshops on health and communication. To my great joy and delight, I learned as much as I shared.

It became apparent to me, over my years of workshops and personal consulting that some people aren't always ready to be introspective. It is either too much trouble to examine innermost feelings, thoughts and motives, or it's simply too scary. Even if these thoughts and motives are destructive, or life threatening, there are people who are simply not interested. Sometimes it takes a wake-up call or major event to jolt us into appreciating how astoundingly fragile, yet powerful we are as human-soul beings.

I am here to tell you that you don't have to experience a major catastrophe to comprehend the significance and power of your thoughts or to understand how this affects every aspect of your life. You can start right now to turn your life around and say "Yes!": Yes! to YOU, Yes! to YOUR LIFE.

Besides changing your mind and perceptions, another key component to saying "Yes!," to Life is your willingness to change your body and therefore your soul and spirit. Some people think that prayer or focused thought is all that is needed to permanently change circumstances. This is a mistake.

What I Learned at The Dojo

I first encountered it the day I decided to get into shape. Haven't we all? I went to a gym, found a trainer who took me through the functions of the different machines. It must have been something I said that launched a conversation about Ki (pronounced *key*) energy or Ki balance. Before I knew it, I'd enrolled in a training class for Aikido (Japanese martial arts) training. For the record, I am an ordinary pudgy, middle-aged woman who has no desire to be slammed on a mat in the name of recreation. Call me Chicken, if you will—it's the truth!

However, my brief time in the dojo did introduce me to the healing power of Kiatsu and a keen awareness of Ki energy. The powerful energy of Ki appears when the mind is not thinking and the body is aligned and centered. This is the energy that enables a sixty-year-old, hundred-pound woman to throw an equally trained, strapping, twenty-year-old, two-hundred-pound man. The secret is *Balance* and that's what Ki energy is all about.

When the mind is not thinking or worrying, the body gains strength and the spirit comes alive with Ki energy. Expressing your true feelings and desires with natural ease and grace become easy. Assertiveness becomes easy.

We've all, at one time or other, wanted to speak up and be assertive. When faced with someone who's impossible to talk to, we'd love to be able to tell that person what we really think. Or when we're fed up with the way our life is going, we want to change harmful behaviors. In each situation, the words have been rehearsed and you've gone over them in your mind many times. The moment arrives, you advance toward the door of true expression and then it happens. Undetectable to the naked eye, tremors of doubts, fears and "what-ifs" course through your veins. Your mouth dries up like the Mohave Desert. Your shallow breathing shoves those rehearsed words past your tongue and over your lips. Meanwhile your body is shouting, "What the hell are you doing?"

It Doesn't Have to Be That Way

I am going to show you an easy, fun way to activate your mind, body and Spirit so that you can live your life's purpose at full potential. Remember, your body, your mind and especially your Spirit are longing for you to wake up, alleviate your tremors of doubt, fear and uneasiness and become the true leader of your life.

It's time to live your optimum life! It is time for your body, mind and spirit to confidently step up with poise and balance and claim what is rightfully yours. It is time to pay attention.

The Ki Exercises throughout this book are designed to awaken the body and therefore the mind and Spirit to a passionate, purposeful life as you learn to communicate your true self.

"The body is so innately connected that if you miss that body/mind connection, then all the other things are hard to tie together."

Dr. Ron Anderson,
Chairman of the Board of Texas Department of Health and
Chief Executive Officer of Parkland Hospital in Dallas Texas

Charlotte Finds Value in "The Snake-charming Hooey"

When I first introduced Ki energy exercises in my health and communication workshops I was astounded at the immediate and effective results experienced by the participants. One woman—we'll call her Charlotte—sat with her arms crossed and her head shaking throughout the first half of the program. I sensed her thoughts: snake-charming hooey, she labeled it. Her body language spoke volumes as the session moved into the role playing session.

Charlotte approached her "difficult situation" with a head-down attitude, as though her thoughts were, "I have worked with this man for fifteen years and nothing is ever going to change." Then we tried something different. I asked her to balance her body and approach her surrogate boss using his body, verbal language and Ki energy.

She took a deep breath, aligned her spine, felt her strength and began to express herself, authentically, clearly and graciously. All the appropriate words and gestures easily fell into place. She confidently approached and connected with a sense of her personal power. An entirely different person metamorphosed before our eyes, as she exclaimed, "Wow, this stuff really works!"

Applying Ki energy to everyday situations creates unlimited applications and possibilities to improve your life, no matter what circumstances you find yourself in today.

If there is a secret or key that has helped me overcome cancer without chemotherapy, radiation and any other invasive treatments, keeping me healthy and happy for over twenty years, it is the utilization of what I am about to share with you in this book.

On these pages I share that secret with you. But this secret comes with a warning. Stop right here! Don't read any further. Put this book down and walk away if you are not willing to put this information to use in your life. I mean it. Walk away if you are not willing to say "Yes!, Yes!, Yes! to life." Let this be the last self-help book you read as you begin the journey of expressing and living an authentic and healthy life.

The Ten Objectives of This Book

On the path to a positive, healthy life, this book will help you:

- Awaken your self-awareness and your unique potential to heal yourself and the world around you.

- Understand personal communication styles so that *oneness* and *commonalities* take priority over *differences* and *separateness*.

- Accept and transcend the scripts and behaviors of the past and remove the roadblocks to expressing your true self.

- Build and increase trust and faith in yourself so you can make a difference in the world.

- Fire up your enthusiasm and boost your optimism.

- Inspire a willingness to do what is right with intention and love.

- Strengthen and affirm your inner courage.

- Create a sense of appreciation and gratefulness that truly empowers life.

- Gain insight so you can create a vision and purpose for your life.

- Experience peace, serenity and a true love for life.

Bringing Ki Energy to Your Daily Life

Ki energy practice is a new concept to the West and an ancient belief in the Eastern half of the world. In this country, it has, however, caught the attention of champion athletes, stockbrokers, successful sale people, executives and homemakers alike.

Bringing Ki energy practice to your daily life amplifies your confidence, determination, your faith in your personal power and when nurtured can have a healing affect on yourself and others. It allows you to be a healthy communicator with coworkers, customers, and family members, thereby creating a healthier more productive and peaceful environment.

This book is designed to guide you to a deeper understanding of yourself and others and help you enliven the body, mind and Spirit. At the end of each chapter I have included *Ki Exercises* to help you do just that. Don't be a couch-potato-reader and expect Ki energy to fly off the page and zap you on the butt. Remember you must experience and practice Ki energy to have it work in your life.

Here's What You'll Find:

In **Chapter One:** *What Part of "Yes!" Don't You Understand?* you will discover the importance of saying YES! to YOUR LIFE. The first step to saying "Yes!" and allowing yourself to grow into a self-healer is awareness. You will learn of the roadblocks and pitfalls that keep you from experiencing the kind of life you want. You'll gain knowledge and understanding of your inalienable rights as a human being, making you aware of your greatness. To help you incorporate this awareness into your daily life, I will introduce you to an easy *Ki exercise.*

In **Chapter Two:** *Will The Amazing You Please Stand Up,* you will gain understanding and reasoning as you explore personality styles in a way you never have before. (Trust me, this is not the usual dry rendition of a personality test.) You will learn valuable insights into each style and you'll become aware of how the different styles intertwine and support one another. The importance of commonalities and differences will become clear. This is fun! The *Ki Exercise* will help you understand just how amazing you really are.

In **Chapter Three:** *Diagonally Parked in A Parallel Universe?* will take you to the next level of applying what you have learned to everyday situations. Explaining the values and effectiveness of each style and how to use this information to effectively improve your communication skills will enable you to understand and really connect with all kinds of people. It will also help you to truly connect with all aspects of your Spirit and what is most important—you. The *Ki Exercise* will further unify your body, mind and Spirit, and will strengthen your resolve.

In **Chapter Four:** *Okay, So What* **Is** *The Speed of Dark?* will help you develop your inner courage and confidence as you begin to make the necessary changes to help you lead the kind of life you want to create. The *Ki Exercise* will help you let go of old fears and relax and begin to accept your new life.

In **Chapter Five:** *All Aboard The "Yes!" Train* will help you understand the power of forgiveness and the importance of dropping old baggage to become a health-promoting communicator. The *Ki Exercise* is designed to drop limiting perceptions and let you move forward.

In **Chapter Six:** *Giving It Up to "Yes!"* you'll discover the power of surrender the various ways to surrender that will help relieve stress and help attract to you the people, places and things to support you in your "Yes!" life. The *Ki Exercise* is designed to help you remember that giving up to Spirit is strength.

In **Chapter Seven:** *My Body Is Not Me, But Mine,* learn the true reason you have a body. Your body is your vessel that gives your soul a place to grow. Learn how to use your body to get the most out of living. The *Ki Exercise* allows you time to get in touch with your divine body and to really appreciate its wonders.

In **Chapter Eight:** *My Mind Is Not Me, But Mine* discover how to utilize the power of your mind to improve your body and mind. Learn how to more effectively use the power tool of your mind to your advantage. The *Ki Exercise* connects your body and mind giving you new insights as you grow closer to the "Yes!" life.

In **Chapter Nine:** *My Soul Is Me And Mine* explores the endless possibilities of what your soul truly desires of you. This is where you can explore your soul's purpose and discover what it is that you can do to make a difference in the world. The *Ki Exercise* deepens your connection to the mind, body and soul allowing you to discover your true self.

In **Chapter Ten:** *The Power Matrix to A "Yes!" Life* culminates all the processes that have been introduced earlier. It will help you to easily access your inner power, connect with your inner self and create a daily practice that's really effective. The *Ki Exercise* will bring you closer to your true Spirit and help you communicate more clearly with yourself and others.

In **Chapter Eleven:** *You Got to be Crazy to Say "Yes!" to Life* will teach you the importance of going a little crazy and trying new ideas. Learn to foster a greater sense of humor while breaking old habits of negative thinking. The *Ki Exercise* will help you rediscover the joy of life.

In **Chapter Twelve:** *The Dream Seekers* will lead you forward, in an exploration of what the purpose of life is really all about.

Leaving Your Comfort Zone

Sometime during your reading of this book I hope that you become very uncomfortable. Yes, you read that correctly—*uncomfortable*—to the point of being moved to stand up for your life. When we are uncomfortable we grow and move toward the change we know we

Here is your chance to explore and appreciate your true, authentic self and how you relate to the world around you. I believe that no one is here by mistake. Everyone is here on this planet Earth for a purpose. You may not know your true purpose yet, but by exploring and understanding yourself and others; your purpose will become clear.

We are all here to make a difference in the lives of others. Even the most dastardly person influences us one way or another. Using your innate communication skills with the balance of Ki Energy, life becomes richer, deeper and more fulfilling. You are a gift to the world. Now is the time to express your gift, authentically and lovingly.

In Love, Grace and Peace,

Judy

Chapter 1

What Part of "Yes" Don't You Understand?

"There is no passion to be found playing small—in settling for a life
that is less than the one you are capable of living."
Nelson Mandela, Civil Rights Leader

Your mother told you, "Just say, No!" No to drugs, sex, rock-n-roll, and chocolate! Was she right? I don't think so. At least not about sex or rock-n-roll, and especially about chocolate. No doubt there are things in life we should say No to, that's a given. However there is one thing our mother neglected to tell us, (actually, she probably never thought about it.) How to say "Yes!" to life?

An ancient Chinese story tells of a worm that crawled through life, eating whatever leaf came his way. Day by day, he struggled to survive in the jungle. Then one day someone told him, "You're not a worm, you're a caterpillar. And caterpillars have potential!" That very day, he began living his life, believing in his potential. He said, "Yes!" to life and his life changed forever, dramatically. He no longer crawled though life trying to survive.

Diligently working toward his goal, he spun a web and attached himself to a strong branch. This was not easy. At times he wanted to quit, yet he kept visualizing his potential. As the cocoon hardened, he took a break from the struggle and surrendered to the comfort of his new home. Then came the day when comfort no longer mattered.

He realized he was much bigger than the world he had created. He thrashed about, trying to make sense of things. Through tremendous pain and discomfort he pressed on. He thought the world was coming to an end; the changes he was going through were dramatic and painful, yet he freed himself from his own limitations. Breathing deeply, he felt his soul blossom with purpose and potential. Yawning and stretching, his beautiful colors emerged; his wings caught the air and he was lifted to a freedom he had only dreamed of. He had truly said, "Yes!" to life.

Inside each of us, in the core of our being, is our soul's desire. It is calling us to awaken our mind, body and spirit, so we can fully experience a blessed life. This book will help you awaken from the "worm mentality" that can keep you in a survival mode, away from true joy and happiness. It is time for you to really understand that you are a soul using a human body form to journey through this lifetime. You have the potential of a butterfly, the power of nature right in your grasp. It's time to stop thinking like the worm. Now it is time to step up to your soul's calling and say, "Yes!"

In the introduction, I related how cancer was my wake-up call, but it doesn't have to be that way for you. Life's experiences, good and bad, support and lead us to the next great event in our lives. In the following chapters, I share the course of action that has helped me to say Yes! to life, and to successfully overcome cancer and stay healthy for over twenty years, without the use of chemotherapy or any other invasive treatment. It is important to note that this process is not a magic pill, nor will reading this book heal you. The only one who can heal and create the healthy happy life you want is *You*.

Like the caterpillar, you will struggle, question the process and, more than likely, resist your own good. That is the nature of being human. Yet real change, real joy and peace never happen without upheaval, confusion, pain or discomfort. Keep telling yourself, *"I can do it,"* and you will.

Start with Awareness

The first step to saying "Yes!" to life is *awareness.* You've probably heard that before, but please take time to stop and really think about it. What is your level of awareness? Of course you're aware of your family, friends, and the guy who cut you off in traffic. You read and watch the news, you have a career of some sort, and some of you might even know today's balance on your bank statement. Now it's time to increase the tempo.

Throughout the next few chapters, we will investigate ways of stretching your level of awareness and opening your soul, mind and body to greater possibilities. Start by asking yourself these questions:

- Do I know what is standing in the way of my truly saying "Yes!" to life?

- How aware am I of the roadblocks that stop me from saying "Yes" and keep me from getting what I want?

- What mode of behavior do I want to utilize in order to change my life?

- What are my inalienable entitlements or rights and how do they affect the quality of my life?

- Am I aware of my life's goals, potential and purpose?

- How aware am I of my conscious and unconscious thoughts, words and actions and their influence on my body, mind and spirit?

- How aware am I of the role my personality style plays in my interaction with myself and others?

Take a moment to ponder each question. Write brief notes as thoughts come to mind. What does this mean? Now, let's look at what is getting in the way of "Yes!" Place a check mark by the roadblocks that ring your bell, strike your gong or twist your knickers.

WHAT GETS IN THE WAY OF "YES"?

Roadblocks to "YES!"

What's holding you back from realizing your potential? Could one of these Roadblocks be keeping you from a more satisfying life?

✥ Roadblock One – Tunnel Vision:

Stemming from our earliest experiences of life we created and perceived our world as in a tunnel. Anything outside of the tunnel is unknown, scary or downright weird and therefore doesn't belong in the tunnel. These antiquated thoughts and beliefs are keeping you from your good.

Having a narrow view point of life will give you a narrow everything: narrow shoulders, narrow vision and narrow arteries. Open up to life by practicing the expansion and stretching of your body and mind and therefore Spirit. The only way out of tunnel vision is to start digging toward the light.

> *"A person will sometimes devote all his life*
> *to the development of one part of the body—the wishbone."*
> Robert Frost

✥ Roadblock Two – Past Thoughts:

Carrying a fifty pound sack of potatoes, slung over one shoulder is comparable to carrying around past thoughts. It's not good for your back and it's throwing you way off balance, but you keep those thoughts churning in your mind unnecessarily. The *should haves, would haves,* and *could haves* will eat you alive if you let them.

Learn to forgive and let go of old grudges or hurtful memories. Embrace the various ups and downs of life as wonderful opportunities to learn and grow. Stop waiting for justice or the day you will be knighted for all your good deeds. IT'S NEVER GOING TO HAPPEN. Only by forgiving yourself and others for past mistakes can you move on.

☯ Roadblock Three – Television:

There's a reason they call it the boob tube, Boob-bee. Don't get me wrong. I have had my share of times when I sat and watched a test pattern, grown square eyes and had a remote control surgically removed from God-knows-where. I'm a confessed Law-head. I am addicted to *Law and Order*, thum-thum. But since my rehab, I have found that television should be taken in small doses.

> *"Television has proved that people will look at anything rather than each other."*
>
> Ann Landers

We are the most informed, *un*informed society in the world. We get our news from sound bites like a McDonald's quarter-pounder-with-a-super-sized-dash-of-ten-second-weather-reports. For God's sake, folks, beware of what you're watching! Are you staring at the same dog food commercial, over and over again—and you don't even have a dog?

The law of attraction is at work even when you are comatose or unconscious. What you are feeding your mind, you are attracting to your life.

☯ Roadblock Four – Very, Very Nice:

There is nothing wrong with being courteous, kind and thoughtful, but being NICE stinks. NICE will kill you. I have watched many of my nice friends die from the disease of NICENESS. Are you nice enough to give away your dreams, relationships and health to please someone else? Nice people are worried about what other people think and they spend too much time trying to please the impossible. So how nice are you?

There is only one person you need to be extremely NICE to: YOU. Begin to pay attention to your mind-set and emotions, and how you feel after you have been NICE. If you feel used, manipulated, or put-upon, you are being way, way too NICE.

☼ Roadblock Five – Brain Dead, Body Dead:

Most people are unaware of the role their body and brain plays in the process of saying "Yes!" to an abundant, healthy life. We know that if you exercise, your body releases endorphins and other power-ful chemicals, which calm the body and, as a result, help you eat less and feel better. But if it were that easy, a whopping sixty percent of Americans would not be extremely overweight.

There has to be more to this. I believe that intense awareness of your body—sensing your body from your nose to your toes—is the key to opening yourself up to a greater understanding of how life works. But your body does not work alone. As you may know, at the core of your being (you can feel this within your body), is an innate energy or Spirit. It is the fire that fuels your life. In various traditions and cultures, the word for energy changes, but no matter what it's called, energy is still energy. I prefer the word *Ki*. When you use the power of Ki to your advantage, your body balances, your brain is enlivened and your life automatically says, "Yes!" You will learn more about this later in the book.

☼ Roadblock Six – Your Choice of Energy:

Everything has and *is* energy. Your words, thoughts and actions are all a form of energy. Therefore every time you speak, think or move, you are using energy. It is your choice of words and thoughts and if you will energy that makes a difference in how your world develops and prospers.

There's a basic concept in physics that says for every action, there is an equal and opposite reaction. We know this universal principal as the *law of attraction*. So if you make the choice to cuss out the driver who cuts in front of you, or if you think of yourself as not "enough," you will continue to attract to you the results of your actions. Choose the way you want to spend your energy as if you were grocery shopping for the finest dinner. What do you want to place on your table for yourself and your guests? Choose the finest words, thoughts, and actions and you will be choosing "Yes!"

✿ Roadblock Seven – An Attitude of Platitude:

So many people in this country of abundance are stressed, pressed and depressed. Why? Instead of thinking of the world as round, abundant and fully packed with life, we tend to see the world as something to trudge through, one dreary step at a time until our heels curl up and our muscles atrophy.

We have more opportunities, prospects, and expectations than other people, living in what we like to call "underdeveloped" countries, or even "developed" countries, for that matter. But are we truly appreciative of what we have? One of the biggest roadblocks to "Yes!" is the simple, yet extremely powerful, phrase, "Thank you." It often seems as if we're waiting to win the lottery, get promoted, or find the perfect relationship before we can be grateful.

This is not how it works, folks. It's the other way around. The more you are grateful for, the more that comes into your life for you to be grateful for. Start by appreciating your family, friends, and the home you rest in. Be grateful for your food, clothing, and job. For God's sake, if nothing else, be truly grateful for your breath. You *are* breathing, aren't you? Well, that's something to be thankful for!

SAY "YES!" TO LIFE

*"If the only prayer you say in your life is thank you,
that would suffice."*

Meister Eckhart

Modes of Behavior

Another way to be more aware of your impact on your world is to ask yourself this: What is my mode of behavior? Examine the following styles of behavior to determine what mode you use most frequently. How do these actions affect the people and situations in your life? Then you might want to ask yourself, as Dr. Phil McGraw would say, "How's that working for ya?"

The Passive Mode

Passive people hope others will give them what they want or need. They need to be liked, and are concerned about how others will judge them and their actions. They usually attract someone who takes over and runs their life for them, or someone who reads minds and has the patience of Job, to wait until they let them know what they want. The only time it's a good idea to be passive is when you are in danger and need to be quiet in order to survive. These people have hardly ever heard of the word YES!

The Aggressive Mode

No patience for anything, it's all about now. With a bulldozer as their main form of transportation, they mow down anyone or anything that gets in the way so they can get their needs met. Generally they attract to them the kind of person who is willing to tolerate this behavior, someone who walks on eggshells or waits until the bulldozer has run out of steam. Aggressiveness is good when something must be done immediately for safety or expedience but not for bullying one's way through life. Aggressive people are trying to say YES! to life but are going to get a big fat NO in their quest for health and happiness.

28

The Passive-Aggressive Mode:

This is a fine barrel of fish. The water in this barrel is swarming with cute little guppies and a man-eating shark. Unfortunately, you never know which one you are going to encounter. Passive-Aggressive people swing from sniping sarcasm to indifference to cordial. They avoid dealing with their feelings of frustration and anger, until they can't stand it any longer—then watch out ... Shark Attack! They attract to them people who love them and don't mind getting bit once in a while. It is hard to say YES! to life when you are unsure what life is going to bring you.

The Assertive Mode

These people see the bigger picture. They are aware of and appreciate other people's differences. They recognize that before they can be assertive with others they have to be assertive with themselves. They weigh the risks and understand the concept of intelligent risk-taking. They function in the workplace and at home as enthusiastic, optimistic motivators and leaders. They encourage others, blame less and think more. Using humor, fairness and energy, they instill trust and a sense of "Good things will happen here." This is where you want to be. This is saying "Yes!" to life.

"Assertiveness is the hub of the wheel of life," states Henry Dreher in *The Immune Power Personality*. He goes on to say, "It influences and empowers careers, relationships, health, and the way we play. It builds our coping skills, gives us a sense of control over our lives, and increases our capacity for pleasure and fun."

Here's Dr. Andrew Salter's definition of assertiveness: "The excitatory person [his preferred term for "assertiveness"] is direct, responding outwardly to their environment. When confronted with a problem, they take immediate constructive action. They sincerely like people, *but they do not care what they may think.* They make rapid decisions, and like responsibility. Above all, the excitatory [assertive] person is free from anxiety."

They Don't Care What Others May Think?

Do you care what others think? Of course you do. We all do. The point that Dr. Salter is making is that the majority of us run our lives on what *other* people think we should say, be, or do. Think back, how many times have you done something simply to gain approval? Or not done something because of what others have said?

My contention is that assertiveness is an innate part of our make-up. We inwardly know when we are being authentic and assertive and when we are not. You have probably experienced this when you've heard yourself say, "Whatever..." or "I don't care," when you didn't really mean it. This is your inner spirit or guidance speaking to you, trying to be heard. The problem is that we are not always willing to listen or trust our inner spirit. There is a way, however, to connect and strengthen our innate assertiveness. It is *Ki Energy*.

Ponder This for A Moment

Which one of these best describes your mode of operation? Do you recognize your mode? Do you recognize those of your family, friends and coworkers? Take a moment to jot down your thoughts. What part of your mode is working for you and what isn't? What part of your behavior would you like to change?

Words, Emotions and Actions that Block "YES!"

My least favorite word is "can't." My granddaughters don't use this word in front of me, because of the involuntarily mini-lecture that launches from my mouth—a bad habit I'm working on. Words, and the emotions and actions they produce, make a difference in how we believe the world to be.

"Words are, of course, the most powerful drug used by mankind."
Rudyard Kipling

Remember, words are powerful forms of energy. To help you understand the impact these words have on your life, take a moment to slowly read the following words out loud, slowly, one at a time. Then ask yourself, "How does that word feel, what emotion does it stir in me?"

How does each word make you feel?

Regret	Can't	Should	Would	Don't know	Tried that
Sorry	Wish	Blame	Wrong	Right	Dumb
Smart	Deny	Ought to	Must	Attack	Shame
Won't	Hide	Put down	Punishment	Threats	Guilt
Separate	Anger	Close	Inactive	Depression	No
Deny	Hate	Punish	Indifferent	Punish	Anxiety

"O Lord, help my words to be gracious and tender
for tomorrow I may have to eat them."
A sign in a restaurant on the Oregon Coast

Phrases that stop the flow of "Yes!"

They did it to me. • I can't get a break. • I hate broccoli.
Maybe I'll do it tomorrow. • Why do I never have enough money?
I can never seem to get ahead. • The world is a scary place.
I don't think I am smart enough. • I tried that once, never again.
"It's a jungle out there," says Adrian Monk.
It never fails to go wrong. • I did it before and it didn't work.
I'm not smart, pretty, or healthy enough.
I just don't feel like doing that.

Know Your Inalienable Rights

Another step on the road to true awareness is consciousness of your personal entitlements or rights. You need to understand that as a human being, just being born is enough. You do not have to be good, nice, sweet, or kind. All you need to know is that you are *entitled*. To assist you in your quest for more "Yeses" in your life, let's take a closer look at your inalienable, personal entitlements.

Read the entitlement out loud. Now consider: How strongly do you believe this statement? You'll be judging the strength of your belief on a scale of one through five:

- One = not hardly
- Two = anything is possible
- Three = that's a nice idea,
- Four = sometimes that works
- Five = that's how I see it.

When you've finished selecting the numbers that best represent the strength of your beliefs in each case, turn the page to tally your score.

"It always seems to me that so few people live—
they just seem to exist—and I don't see any reason
why we shouldn't LIVE always—
till we die physically—
why do we do it all in our teens and twenties...?
Georgia O'Keefe

Personal Entitlement Quiz

1. I am entitled to be paid fairly for what I do.
   1   2   3   4   5

2. I am entitled to succeed. I am entitled to fail.
   1   2   3   4   5

3. I am entitled to go against what others think.
   1   2   3   4   5

4. I am entitled to be different from what others expect me to be.
   1   2   3   4   5

5. I am entitled to have great relationships even with those who bug me?
   1   2   3   4   5

6. I am entitled to look in the mirror, naked or not and like what I see.
   1   2   3   4   5

7. I am entitled to use my natural healing and self-healing abilities.
   1   2   3   4   5

8. I am entitled to celebrate my worth based on my own standards.
   1   2   3   4   5

9. I am entitled to express my feelings and opinions.
   1   2   3   4   5

10. I am entitled to say "No" without feeling guilty.
    1   2   3   4   5

11. I am entitled to be listened to and taken seriously.
    1   2   3   4   5

12. I am entitled to meet my needs and/or ask to have my needs met.
    1   2   3   4   5

13. I am entitled to be treated with respect.
    1   2   3   4   5

14. I am entitled to try anything, if I will accept the consequences.
    1   2   3   4   5

15. I am entitled to design my life any way I want to.
    1   2   3   4   5

TALLY YOUR RIGHTS - Scoring Chart					
	1	2	3	4	5
Statement # 1:					
Statement #2:					
Statement #3:					
Statement #4:					
Statement #5:					
Statement #6:					
Statement #7:					
Statement #8:					
Statement #9:					
Statement #10:					
Statement #11:					
Statement #12:					
Statement #13:					
Statement #14:					
Statement #15:					
Totals:					

Analyzing The Results

Now let's take a look at your tally. Of course, if you have all fives, you can close this book and go home. But most of us are going to have entitlements we are either unaware of, or ones we are still working on. Either way, this quiz will give you some idea where to start and will illustrate what may be keeping you from the success you want.

Ask yourself:

- What entitlements would help me increase my income?
- What entitlements could I exercise more to create meaningful relationships?
- What entitlements will help me express myself more clearly?
- What entitlements could I exercise to help me deal with weight issues and health?
- What entitlements would help me hone my leadership skills?

What Gets in the Way of "YES!"

❧ Using abstract terms: "You always." Or "I can't do that."

❧ Guessing at the other person's motive or goals: "He'll say this and I'll do that and..."

❧ Denying your feelings: "That's all right; it doesn't matter to me."

❧ Not making make eye contact.

❧ Being short and appearing uncaring, to get something done.

❧ Going to the next venture without appreciation for what has been accomplished.

❧ Forgetting to center yourself in Ki energy before you begin any new task.

❧ Using confusing body language.

❧ Attacking the character of the person.

❧ Ignoring the other person's needs or asking only for your satisfaction.

❧ Making exaggerated threats or unrealistic threats.

❧ Using self-defeating language to yourself and others.

❧ Thinking the other person is the only person who has to change.

❧ Using indirect directives: "Will *someone* get the phone?"

❧ Unleashing emotional outbursts.

Words and Actions to Lead to Yes

Try adding these YES! words to your daily conversations. Take a deep breath and let it out. Sit with each of these words and ask yourself what they mean to you. How do they feel when you read or hear them? You can muscle test yourself by connecting your thumb and first finger to create a chain. Say the word out loud. Now hold them tight and try to pull them apart. If they come apart easily, your energy or belief about that word is not strong. Repeat the word until you feel comfortable with it or find another word to energy test.

Practicing YES! Words

Courage	Perfect	Love	Neutrality	Accept	Joy
Harmony	Wise	Oneness	Complete	Enough	Inspire
Yes	Willing	Can	Happy	Smile	Movement
Together	Expand	Open	Reverence	Heal	Acceptance
Mend	Confront	Fairness	Flow	Calm	Peace
Merciful	Satisfied	Whole	Reason	Forgive	Understand

"Talk doesn't cook rice."

Chinese Proverb

It is one thing to learn about roadblocks, modes of behavior and the power of words and quite another to put them into action. Take for instance my friend, Agnes, from Seattle.

Clueless in Seattle

Agnes loved her job. As a counselor for Washington Family Home Visits she found her position very rewarding. Every client she helped taught her something about herself. Although this job was new to her, she was confident in her ability. That is, until she met the Normans. They had her stumped. Each visit had the smiles, charms and grace of a "Leave it to Beaver," episode. Donna, Jim and their teenage son Todd were at a stalemate. No one was talking and no one was listening. Agnes offered wise advice and constructive ideas. She suggested asking open-ended questions and listening for solutions, but none of this was enough to break the deadlock.

Frustrated, Agnes suggested that at their next meeting everyone should relax and become a little more laid back. "Don't bother to get dressed up, just wear what you usually wear," she added, as she exited through their front door.

That next week, Agnes was greeted at the door. "Donna! Agnes is here!" called Jim as he tucked his grungy tank top into his boxer shorts and invited her in. Donna smiled hello and fluffed her pink negligee over her ample body. Then Todd moseyed into the front room, wrapped in a wet towel. Agnes found a chair because by then she needed one.

Agnes wasn't at all sure what to do next. Do I laugh, or just act as if nothing has happened? She stifled her laughter and decided to go with the flow. Whatever will be, will be, she thought. Straightening her spine, she took a deep breath and centered herself. She remembered her purpose, aligned herself with Ki energy and dropped her preconceived notion of how this session would go. Looking around the room of half naked people, she decided to be aware and keep her thoughts in the moment.

Time passed quickly as the session filled with questions and discussions that seem to go nowhere. Pink feathers and boxer shorts pushed at her purpose. Agnes didn't show her disappointment, but it was there nevertheless, as she firmed up the time for the next meeting and said her good-byes.

Feeling the Agnes of defeat (the pun is intended) she sighed, slipped into her Dodge Dart, turned the key and wondered where she had gone wrong. What could she have done differently? And was there any hope for the Normans? She began to feel that it was unlikely she could ever break through that barrier.

Then one last glance at the Norman's front window changed everything. Silhouetted in a golden orange glow were three people in their underwear hugging and smiling—the loving family they were intended to be.

Agnes' story is an example of how saying "Yes!" to a different approach, allowing yourself to do something out of the ordinary, changes the energy and spirit of everyone involved. It is about opening the mind to greater possibilities and letting go of ingrained expectations of the outcome.

An Essential Element to "Yes!"

It is essential, before we go any further, that you understand the extent to which I want you to stretch your awareness and understanding of the world around you. You have investigated the roadblock, modes of behavior, words that block "Yes!" and words that bring "Yes!" You've squarely looked at your entitlements or rights and thereby evaluated your level of awareness. Now let me explain the element that is crucial to the entire process of you saying "Yes!" to life and leading the kind of life you dream of.

The Element is Ki Energy

The earth on which you live, as well as you, your friends, family and every other material thing are the results of evolutionary changes through which microscopic bits of matter have been organized and arranged in an orderly fashion. Every one of the billions of individual cells of your body and every atom of matter is an intangible form of energy. Science has revealed that this energy is in and through all things. And as you travel throughout the world, you'll find there are many names for this energy: *Chi, Qi, Shakti, Spirit, God* and dozens of others that describe the inner spirit.

Aikido and other martial arts practices describe Ki as, "The universal innate energy within a person." This five-thousand-year-old ancient Samurai practice teaches people how to rise above self-love, to reach a level of love and respect for humanity and society, all the while benefiting the practitioner. All people have Ki energy, even if they are not aware of it. It is the core of who we are. It gives you balance and strength. It is the invisible spirit within; it is the glue of our existence.

I first encountered the practice of Ki energy was when I visited a Japanese dojo to take Aikido (martial arts) training. I didn't mind getting thrown through air, but it was the landing I had a problem with. I never did get the hang of it, yet I was fascinated to realize that students were not using physical strength alone to throw their opponents, but the balance of Ki energy.

Energy in Any Language is Still Energy

There are many words you substitute for the word *Ki*. Various religions, marital arts and meditation practices have developed different words for Ki energy yet it is the energy not the word that is important.

Country:	Energy Word:
Japan	Ki Energy
Korea	Ki Energy
China	Chi or Qi Energy
India	Shakti Energy
USA	Spirit or God Energy

These words have different meanings for different people and yet energy is energy.

Ki Exercise # 1

Because breath is so important to your body; take in a deep breath and then let it out. Turn on some soft music and lie down comfortably. Take a moment to feel your body settle in. Notice how it slowly releases and lets go of the cares of the day. Let go of all thoughts and stay focused on what your body is communicating.

Imagine a ball of healing light around your toes. Feel its warmth as it soothes and relaxes. Now let the ball of healing light slowly permeate you legs… knees… thighs…hips… stomach… back…chest…arms…neck and face. Slowly your body relaxes into the moment. Stop thinking… give yourself this special gift of time.

Take a deep breath and let it out. Take a moment to become accustom to loving yourself just the way you are right now. Now focus on the center point of Ki energy; it is an invisible spot just below your belly button. Place both hands on this area and breath into your Ki energy center. Breathe in, hold the breath then let it out. Do this twenty times. Your energy builds as you become aware or conscious of your body and its subtle yet powerful and renewable energy.

It is time to let go of roadblocks of old stagnant beliefs and perceptions and stand up for your soul's purpose. It is time to appreciate the power of your behavior and entitlements and the power of your thoughts. It is time to open your mind, body and Spirit to a broader more abundant and prosperous life. It is time to say "Yes."

Chapter 2

Will The Real YOU Please Stand Up?

"You are the greatest miracle in the world."

Og Mandino

Well, let's get right down to it. If you really knew how amazing you really are you would be overwhelmed and you'd burst at the seams with joy. Every aspect of you is utterly and totally amazing. Take your brain, for instance. This lump between your shoulders is more than just something for your neck to hold up.

Your brain is the most complex structure in the universe. Within its three pounds are over thirteen billion nerve cells, more than three times as many cells as there are people on the earth. Their purpose is to help you file away every perception, every sound, every taste, every smell and every action you have experienced since the day of your birth. Within your cells are implanted more than one thousand billion, billion protein molecules.

Every incident in your life is there, waiting only your recall. And to assist your brain in the control of your body there are dispersed, throughout your form, four million pain-sensitive structures, five hundred thousand touch detectors and more than two hundred thousand temperature detectors. Now that's what I call protection and guidance. The fact is, within you is enough atomic energy to light a great city or to destroy it.

Your amazing brain not only manages all body functions, stores memories, but also has the capability of healing itself by growing new neurons to support new thoughts and new ideas. I told you, you are *amazing*!

A New-Fangled Personality Test!

Another step on the road to true awareness is a personality test, but before you groan, hear this! I know you're saying to yourself "I been there, done that and I ain't going back there again." However my version is anything but "Ye Olde Personality Test" and I guarantee you'll not only enjoy it, but you'll learn a great deal.

For a moment, think back to those personality tests of yore. Let me ask you, what did you learn from these tests? Have you been able to implement this information into your daily life? Has it helped you begin to heal yourself or lead a more satisfying life? Well, this one should do just that.

You probably never thought of personality traits in this way before. Yet there is so much you can reap from this knowledge. The following *Positive Perceptions Profile* and the explanations that follow are designed to give you a deeper understand of just how amazing and intrinsic your personality is to your well-being. I'll show you how to use this information to heal and make whole everyday real-life situations that are troubling you and bringing you "*dis*-ease."

Please follow the directions for the *Positive Perceptions Profile* exercise. As you read the description of each personality style, see if you recognize these various unique and valuable characteristics in yourself, friends and family.

"I have nothing to declare but my genius."
Oscar Wilde

Positive Perceptions Profile

First we'll start with your own personality and later on, you can evaluate the personality traits of family and friends by sharing this profile with them.

Consider the first horizontal row of four words, then place a score of 4, 3, 2, or 1 in the space in front of each word, with the numbers ranging from 4 being *most like you* to 1 being *least like you*. Which of the four traits do you value most? For example, in a conversation with another person, do you appreciate *accuracy* or *friendliness*? Do you appreciate someone who is *direct*, or is *patience* a very important characteristic?

Continue down the list, taking each group of four words at a time, rank each word by putting a number (1 to 4) in the space in front of it. Total the columns vertically and write the total on the space provided.

Positive Perceptions Profile			
__ Patient	__ Accurate	__ Direct	__ Friendly
__ Loyal	__ Systematic	__ Adventurous	__ Persuasive
__ Passive	__ Judgmental	__ Stubborn	__ Impulsive
__ Neighborly	__ Competent	__ Self-Reliant	__ Confident
__ Gentle	__ Conventional	__ Forceful	__ Optimistic
__ Even-tempered	__ Restrained	__ Quick	__ Colorful
__ Predictable	__ Practical	__ Outspoken	__ Emotional
__ Easy mark	__ Perfectionist	__ Impatient	__ Talkative
__ Good listener	__ Law-abiding	__ Self-directed	__ High-spirited
__ Content	__ Cautious	__ Risk-taker	__ Playful
__ TOTAL	__ TOTAL	__ TOTAL	__ TOTAL

Now transfer your scores for each column to the chart below:

Tally Your Scores:			
Column 1	Column 2	Column 3	Column 4
Total:	Total:	Total:	Total:
Your type is:	Your type is:	Your type is:	Your type is:
BLUE	GREEN	RED	YELLOW

Now, that you have completed the test, check the totals for your highest score and the color below it. Blue is in the first column, Green in the second, Red in the third, and Yellow in the fourth column.

If you have completed the test correctly your highest score will reflect your dominate communication style. (If you have tied scores, that's fine; make a note of those two or more colors.)

Your Dominant Communication Style

When you begin to write, tie your shoes or brush you teeth, you use your dominate hand. The same is true of your dominant communication style. This is the style you are most familiar with. It is how you like to start a conversation and, more than likely, this style colors (for lack of a better word) your entire perception of life. You are comfortable with this style and you believe that the world would be a better place if everyone communicated the way you do. "*We would all get along so much better if everyone was like me.*" But that's not how it works.

In the real world, everything is made up of different colors, hues and shades. Nature demonstrates this in the sky, flowers, mountains, trees and people. As a prism reflects, separates and displays a variety of colors from one single source, so does each person project varying amounts of all colors from the One Source within. This ironically makes us all the same and all different from each other. This reflection happens all the time, even when we are not aware of it. The secret is to use these color personality styles, which are at your disposal every moment, to achieve a sense of balance and equilibrium when trying to understand yourself and your dealings with others.

See if you recognize your friends, spouse, coworkers, boss or children in the following descriptions. Notice commonalities and appreciate the many unique approaches to living life. Keep an open mind as you read each description to gain a deeper understanding of how your relationship with yourself and others works or doesn't work.

From Judy's Notebook:
Your favorite color or dominant color style is influenced by your
environment; career, politics, culture, family history and financial
status. Or just maybe it was decided when you incarnated
on this planet. I can't scientifically prove it, but it does explain
why my forest Green daughter, Susan, from the first day she could
walk, tried to organize my life, and Ron, my son, who's Red,
obtained the nickname "Bam-Bam" at a very young age.

Positive Perception of Styles

A Description of Color Characteristics

As I said before, we have all four personality color styles at our disposal. If you want to be the leader of your life, heal your mind and body and declare what you want and get it, you must understand the power of your personality and use this information to your best advantage.

"All leaders have their own style. Great leaders are authentic or real. They have the ability to let people know who they really are."

Bill Harrison, CEO, J.P. Morgan/Chase

Let's take a look at the different styles:

Blue

The "Blue" Style Is Relationship-Oriented

When a Blue walks into the world, walks into a room, or engages in conversation, they smile and warmly say to themselves, "Is there going to be a relationship here?" Their eyes scan the room, searching for ways to relate or connect.

Blue is vital to a person's well being. It is the part of you that knows that peace and calmness will heal anything. Without it, you cannot love yourself or others. Without Blue, a balanced world would not exist. Here are characteristics of Blues:

❧ **Steadfastly loyal,** Blues will stand by a cause, marriage or organization with unwavering loyalty. Of course this can sometimes be detrimental to their health. Their ability to make people feel comfortable, gain their trust while maintaining integrity and fairness creates loyalty and is an important Blue strength. To a Blue their word is their bond and they expect the same from you. The strong point of loyalty will help you as you focus on your goals and aspirations for a better life.

❧ **Speaking indirectly**—as Blues are prone to do—allows the listener to be drawn into and included in a conversation. It forms a consensus and a "for the good of all" feeling.

Have you ever overheard two blues going to lunch? It goes like this:

"Where do you want to go?"

"I don't know,"

"I don't know. Where do you think we could go?"

"I don't know."

"Where do *you* want to go?"

Get a grip! Can't you make up your mind? The thing is, you see, Blues don't really care where they go to lunch. It just has to be a place where they can create relationships. It's all about nurturing the relationship. It's all about nurturing you.

❧ **Intuitive Nature.** Blue's intuitive nature gives them the capacity to read people. They do this by creating direct eye contact. It's said that the eyes are the window to the soul. When Blues are looking into your eyes they are reading your soul where there is a true sense of who you are. They are deciding how much relationship material can be tossed into the conversation and what they ought to leave out. They are deciding if you are a person they can trust with their feelings. A Blue's intuition is a powerful tool in the healing process because it is the Blue part of us that knows love is all there is.

❧ **Peace Keepers.** At the first sign of conflict, shoulders go up, eyeballs pop, heads spin and Blues head for the door. It can be a raised voice or some loud pushy person, but they will be gone instantly, either mentally or physically. It's not so much that they are afraid. They just don't see a reason for conflict. They believe that the world would be a better place if we all got along. They will do what they can to negotiate a settlement rather than create the slightest hint of disagreement. Now, that's not a bad idea when you consider the state of the world right now. Recognize the need for peace within you? Thank God for peace keepers. They're definitely Blue.

❧ **Enjoy People.** A one-on-one personal conversation really gets the Blue's juices cooking. They enjoy people in a rich and rewarding interpersonal way. There is a great deal of disease when a Blue doesn't have a feeling of connectedness in a personal relationship, Using indirect language, direct eye contact, details and niceties will deepen relationships, heal bodies and mend bridges. Some people ask "what's the point of all those details and warm fuzzy stuff in a conversation?" The point is, there is no point. Sometimes, a conversation is only about learning how best to serve others.

Blue's Motto:

A smile makes the world a better place.

Green

The Green Style is Project-Oriented

When a Green engages in conversation or observes the world around them, they are taking notice of people, places and things as they contemplate "the project." If they can hang their hat on a project, organize it and analyze it, they have imparted a sense of true meaning to their life. The Green part of our personality gives us a starting point and a goal as we set our minds on change. It helps us to organize our thoughts to see the sequence of life and decide how we can change it when we want to. Without Green in our personality, we would never complete anything and a balanced world would not exist.

When people with a dominant Green style are having a conversation with you, they are asking themselves three questions:

- How much time is this going to take?

- Am I wasting my time?

- How much time do I need to finish?

Do I make myself clear? Green is all about time. Because of their keen sense of timing they accomplish things faster and more efficiently than other personality styles.

Analytical and Methodical by Nature, Greens have a broad view of a company, organization or a personal relationship. It is this overview that helps them stay objective, open minded and ready to solve problems quickly and efficiently. Weighing their options, analyzing the situation and forming a plan may appear indecisive. Yet this is what saves time; increases productivity and gives measure to any healing process. This is where prioritizing will help you create a life-changing plan for your life.

The Green Zone: "Wait a minute," Says the Green, without even looking up. They continue reading; a hand flies up like the white glove of a traffic cop. When they've finished reading they reply, "So, what did you want?"

Welcome to the twilight of the Green Zone, where time reigns. Greens may appear impolite or it may seem that they just don't care. The simple truth is, if they don't read the entire page before they talk with you, they will lose the gist of the page and have to read it again from the beginning. This would take more time. This strong sense of focus helps the Green part of you reach your objective immediately.

Time-Conscious, You Think? Greens don't like you to waste their time, but they don't mind wasting their own time. My Green friend, Sandy, and I went camping together in the San Juan Islands off the coast of Washington State. She had been there before and wanted to share with me her love of this gorgeous country.

"All you'll need is your sleeping bag, I'll pick you up at 8:00 AM," said Ms. Green.

Precisely at 8:00 AM I closed Sandy's car door and was handed the itinerary. It looked something like this:

Day One-

8:00 AM: Pick up Judy

11:30 AM: Arrive at the Ferry

12:00 PM: Eat Lunch

1:00 PM: Tour Historical Church and Graveyard

2:00 PM: Set up Camp/Sea Lions and Whale Viewing

Day Two- .... Need I need to go on?

Remember when you were a kid, and the balloon you were blowing up got away from you, flapping willy-nilly in the air before you could get a knot in it? That's the sound my brain was making as I read the list. I didn't say anything at the time but I could feel my fun escaping like so much hot air. Why would you go to the trouble of making a list? We were going on vacation, for God's sake.

But here's what I learned from this: Sandy thoughtfully planned our time so we wouldn't be late for the ferry crossing. If we had been late we would have had to wait two hours for the next one. Once we were on the islands the itinerary loosened up and, in fact, went away. Because of Ms.Green's list we had a wonderful relaxing vacation.

Private People. Greens become so enthralled with their project that they hardly come up for air, let alone relationships. In the 1990s, it wasn't uncommon for a company to be bought and sold more often than Elizabeth Taylor had husbands. A client of mine worked for five dot com companies in five years and never moved from his desk. Eric constantly looked over his shoulder for the one morning he would be handed his pink slip. That morning finally came.

Without notice, Eric found himself out of a job. He was befuddled. What happened? He was extremely good at his job and he knew it, but why was *he* being let go? His supervisor explained. "We discussed letting you go at last week's meeting," he went on, "I told them it was out of the question because you always get the job done faster and more efficiently than anyone I know. I will straighten this out, but my advice to you is to let people know what you do by sending an e-mail or memo. You don't have to brag, just make your presence known." Good advice, Greens. (My advice: let people know who you really are.)

Appreciates Order And A Good List. Greens are fired up with a list. If you want to make a point, and check it for clarity, have a Green listen to your idea. Be considerate of his or her time, do your best to appear organized and bring a **LIST**. Okay, so some of us have never made a list. But go ahead; just make a list for the Greens in your life. Something so little will mean so much.

Incidentally, **ORDER** does not mean *neat*. Order is something that's firmly implanted in the head of a Green. The next time you are in a Green's office start your conversation, then pick up something off the desk and begin swinging it around as you talk. Watch Green's eyes follow the object up and down and all around. Then put it down in a different place. You have just rattled a Green's cage big time. "You've moved my thing," shivers down the Green's spine. They can't wait until the object is in its rightful place. This may appear unreasonably obsessive but the truth is, there's a little mechanism in the brain that believes order on the smallest scale saves time. And beside, this *is* their stuff, after all. Use this helpful trait to keep your balance as you work through the nature of chaos or disruption.

Green's Motto:

Leave me alone, I can do it better by myself.

Red

The "Red" Style is Goal-Oriented

A laser beam aimed at a goal is the way Reds perceive their world. Their uncanny focus and determination is the hallmark of all successful ventures. Once they have made up their mind about something, nothing will stand in the way of accomplishing it. This unique intensity moves things forward steadfastly and without doubt. The tenacity, self-confidence and determination of the Red will help you stay on task and go through whatever pain or discomfort you must to develop the kind of life you want. The world would not be balanced without the strengths of Red.

Appear Abrupt. Reds appear abrupt? No question about it. A Red has a semi-automatic tongue that shoots from the hip. They see things in a linear fashion: everything is a straight line to somewhere. They come right to the point, say what they mean and often wonder why everyone else can't do the same. Reds are not interested in frivolous details and niceties unless it will help get them where they want to go. As you can tell, Blues and Reds differ: Blues love details, Reds don't see a need. This is where Reds appear abrupt or uncaring. Don't take it personally. It's about fire in the belly, reaching the goal determination. This is what you will need if you want to succeed.

People are Resources. There is no such thing as small talk to a Red. Anything that appears to be small talk is an information-gathering endeavor. Just below the skin of a Red's skull is a Rolodex. What's your name? What do you do? How successful are you? Can I get your business card? (Notice it's not about weather or the folks.) They are filling their filing system with information. The next time they need a bricklayer they'll know where to go. This may appear cold and uncaring to some, but keep in mind the importance of knowing where to go and what to use to solve difficult situations or challenges. This could save your life.

❧ **Target Your Intention.**

"When your attention is aligned with your intention, nothing can stop you from having what you want...except doubt."

Dr. Deepak Chopra

A Red knows this better than anyone. To achieve results you must take careful aim, avoid possible obstacles and shoot with a purpose. Reds are driven by purpose and know that the only way to get what they want is to direct and focus their thinking toward their intended goal. If you have a target or goal, something you want to accomplish, take time each day to imagine yourself reaching it.

❧ **Highly Competitive.** Red's office walls are lined with awards, trophies, conquests and achievements. Contrast this to a Blue, who plays a game of golf for fun. Reds believe the game was invented solely for them to win. They love competition, but most of all they enjoy competing against themselves. This competitive nature makes them risk-takers and they demonstrate a willingness to go for the whole enchilada. Not willing to settle for second place, they strive to be the best, have the best, and live the best they can. Red is an unquestionable asset when you want to live a life of abundance, love and peace.

❧ **Constructive Banter?** Like an Italian cook with steaming spaghetti, Reds love to throw around ideas and see which ones stick to the wall. They like to call it "constructive banter," while others might say they were arguing. Reds will never be caught short for an opinion and will question anything that seems to be unclear to them. This consensus-gathering tool is quite useful when it comes to asking and receiving care and attention. Being able to stand up and ask the right questions is empowering and will boost your self confidence.

Red's Mottoes:

1. I want it done NOW

2. The game is on and the Reds are going to win!

Yellow

The Yellow Style Is Fun-oriented

"Where's The Party?!!" Yellows are always looking for the party side of life. If they show up, there must be a party. This is the fun, creative, imaginative, lighter side of our selves. Yellow's fun loving quality keeps us sane and talks us down from the ledge when life gets too serious. You will not be figuring out your checkbook, making a list or, for that matter, doing much of a serious nature when you are in the Yellow Zone.

The paradoxical part: Yellows have a tendency to have fun to excess and even to their own demise. On the other hand, the Yellow Zone is where you are most in touch with your inner self or your intuitive nature. It is the channel by which you access your Spiritual strength.

Levity Seekers. The next time you attend a board (or bored) meeting take a moment to look around at all the color styles at the table. The Reds have brought the issue; the Blues have made sure there is paper, pencils, water and cups, as the Greens tap their nails, waiting for "the project," the meeting drags on. Everyone has input their input. The Yellow's eyes begin to glaze over, they have listened long enough. Then they turn to you and say, "Did you hear the one about ..." Everyone laughs, then it's back to the business at hand. So it goes in life; when we get too serious, we are saved by the humor bell.

Freeform Thinkers. Thinking outside the box? What box? Yellows don't need no stink'n box. Your Yellow imagination is unlimited. It is where all possibilities lie. When you are in your Yellow Zone, hundreds of ideas fly in and out, moment to moment. If it weren't for the other colors and their stabilizing effects, you would be overwhelmed. The good thing about freeform thinking is that if you have an idea and don't like it, just wait a minute and another one will come along. Nothing is solid or concrete. It's all in *What-If Land*, where new concepts and ideas can be played and spent. There is no need for a LIST here. This is where the mind meets its true self and possibilities of healing are created.

※ **Highly Intuitive.** Intuitively, Yellows have a visceral sense of energy, when they are aware of it. It is a sense that energy is all around them, waiting to be used. Clairvoyants, psychics, and artists of all kinds draw from this highly-developed intuition and you can too. Developing and trusting your intuition is key to improving any aspect of your life. You will be able to intuitively sense whether a person, place or thing is good for you or not. You can avoid a lot of trouble when you are in tune with your intuition.

※ **Leaving Their Droppings.** The next time you are at a party, take a gander at all the different colors. Blues: Over near the food table, gathering relationships. Greens: calculating the appropriate time they can leave the party. Reds: Sitting side-by-side, shooting words and bobbing their heads. The Yellow finches: Flitting from one person to another, laughing, joking and what I call affectionately leaving their droppings. They're dropping off a little joy here and there as they decide who's going to be the most fun. By being appreciative and aware of this quality, you can understand how beneficial this can be as you create droppings of love and understanding in your world.

※ **In The Yellow Zone: Out And Happy About it.** The Yellow Zone is way, way, way out there in Never, Never Land. Or Always, Always Land. This is the *Land of What If*, where anything is possible. This is where we go when we want to recharge and rejuvenate our lives. When we are in the Yellow Zone we know tomorrow will be a better day. Our daydreams and imaginations run wild here. We are most child-like in our Yellow Zone. Abandoning our fears and doubts we live spontaneously on possibilities. As children are pleased with themselves, so it is we are happy with whom we are, just the way we are at the moment. This is the creative nature of self-healing and that is what knowing your true self is all about.

Yellow's Motto:

"If it's not fun, I'm not doing it."

Gather Your Thoughts

Take a moment to reflect on what you have learned so far. Has this exercise changed your perception of yourself and others? Do you see more of the commonalities than the differences and separateness? Take a moment to list three things that you have learned from this chapter:

1. _____

2. _____

3. _____

The Amazing You and Your Four Colors

The amazing you has all four color styles. Each one is an intricate part of your personality. I wager to say that you would not survive in this world without using all four color styles in your daily life. Just think about taking away one element, say Green, out of your personality. Now, you would use your friendly Blue, spearheaded Red and fun-loving Yellow, but would be unable to complete the smallest of tasks. If you tossed out your Red you would live in a pool of unresolved, uncertainty. You would be Blue, if your Blue was unable to have relationships. And forget even talking to you if you have no fun Yellow. Each color style supports the other and adds unique value to your life.

Something to Think About

Imagine the first committee to build a bridge. All four colors stood on the river's shore. First to speak was the Yellow. "I have this idea, let's build a bridge!"

Caught up in the enthusiasm of the Yellow, the Red says, "Yes… what's a bridge?"

The Green starts, "Let's make me a list."

"I'll go talk to folks and see what the consensus is," says the Blue.

The point is, that without each of these colors and innate talents and balance we would still be living in the stone age, without a bridge or a pot to put it in. These personality styles give us the ability to live productive balanced lives.

You are amazing and unique. Your dominant personality style is your exclusive view of the world. Understanding the value and appreciating the intricate way these colors are woven into everything you do and say will help you to understand yourself and others.

In the next chapter we'll explore how to best use your personality style to express your true self and attract to you the success and happiness you want.

Resource Center

The personality color styles I've developed have been gathered from a myriad of sources, shoved in a blender, and given a pinch of common sense for effective use in everyday situations. These resources are among my favorites:

- *The Essential Enneagram: The Definitive Personality Test and Self-Discovery Guide*, by David Daniels, M.D. is a simple and accurate way to identify your Enneagram personlity type and to assist you in furthering you personal and professional development.
- www.personality100.com
- www.personalitydesk.com

Ki Exercise # 2

Switch on some soft, comforting music as you take time to be with your beautiful and amazing self. Breathe deeply and let it out. Let your body relax and balance itself right where you are right now. Draw in a deep cleansing breath and release it fully. Relax your shoulders and close your eyes. Let your entire body go limp.

Take another deep refreshing breath. As you gather new positive energy into your body and mind, focus on your center point or Ki energy point (just below your belly button). As you breathe in, you gather strength, and as you release your breath you allow new energy, new ideas and behaviors to be attracted to you.

Let go of any thoughts, worries or concerns. Let your mind drift as you imagine yourself on a garden path. As you walk along the path notice, off to one side, a small pond that reflects all the beautiful colors in nature. A Blue sky pours over Green abundant plant life. Everywhere you are, there is color. Relax and take time to observe the minutest details: the Red tree sap crystals glistening as Yellow Buttercups dance with delight.

All people, places and things are made up of these colors, these subtle yet powerful energies. Every color is present in all and therefore there should be no place for you to create separatism, discrimination or hate. No one is better than you. You are no better than anyone else. Everyone is unique and amazing in their choice of life style. Take a deep breath and let joy fill your heart. Let gratitude and appreciation flow through you as you realize your oneness with nature and your oneness with every human being on the earth. Breathe in your amazing-ness. Breathe in oneness for all.

Chapter 3

Diagonally Parked in A Parallel Universe?

"Human contribution is the essential ingredient.
It is only in the giving of oneself to others that we truly live."
Ethel Percy Andrus

$\mathcal{H}$ave you ever had one of those days where things just kept slipping sideways while you tried to get a grip? Unless you are from Uranus or some other port, you know what I'm talking about, especially when it comes to conversations.

There's the *Wham Bam Thank You, Mam* exchange, whereby words are tossed back and forth, leaving you wishing you had gotten your point across and been understood. Maybe you've encountered the person who never has time, who hands off words on the run and gives you what I call the W*here's the Door* chat that's got you frustrated. Either way, these exchanges fall flat on the floor with all the other dead conversations and get swept into oblivion.

These sideways conversations lead to complacency, a general acceptance that this is the way it is and nothing can change it. It's easy to underestimate the cost this has on our self-esteem and universal enthusiasm for life. As I stated early, "Assertiveness is the hub of life." It affects every aspect of your life; your personal and professional relationships, finances, and most definitely your health and sense of well-being. Yet, assertive communication is not taught or encouraged as a life skill in our schools or culture.

Understanding and becoming consciously aware of the various ways in which you express yourself, such as body language, vocal tones and how you deal with fear, will give you insight into a type of communication that not only gets you to "Yes!" but also increases your ability to self heal.

In the following exercises, a *Positive Perceptions Color Matrix*, take time to evaluate what it is you appreciate about your personality style and what you would like to change. You will need to be aware of each color's body language and how this affects the continuity and harmony of a conversation.

Positive Perceptions Color Matrix

1. In pursuit of deeper self-awareness, list at least five of the best characteristics of your color style.

   1. _____

   2. _____

   3. _____

   4. _____

   5. _____

2. What advantages do you see in balancing your use of the different personality styles to increase your ability to create peace and heal your life?

_____

_____

3. What are some of the characteristics of your color style that you don't like?

_____

_____

4. What aspects of your color style could you soften or strengthen, and why?

_____

_____

5. What color style(s) would you like to integrate, in order to be a more effective communicator, and why?

_____

_____

6. In your quest to understand yourself and other people better, what is the most difficult color style for you to communicate with, and why?

_____

_____

7. What do you appreciate about the different color styles? How do these styles support you when communicating with others?

Blue _____

Green _____

Red _____

Yellow _____

8. What could you introduce into your life to help you focus or center yourself and thereby generate strength and confidence?

Meditation _____   Visualization _____

Relaxation _____   Other _____

9. What starting sentence would be most effective when communicating with each color? Match the appropriate color—Blue, Green, Red, or Yellow—to each of the following sentences:

    a. "I know how important your time is..." _____

    b. "Hi, how are you doing?" _____

    c. "This is the bottom line..." _____

    d. "This is going to be fun." _____

10. When approaching a particular color style with criticism, what statement would be most effective when communicating with a Blue, Green, Red or Yellow? Write your answer after the sentence.

    a. "Let me come right to the point..." _____

    b. "You must have put in a lot of time on this" _____

    c. "Wow, you're so creative and fun..." _____

    d. "You have done such a *nice* job..." _____

Here's Help If You Need It...

You are on your own in answering the first seven questions. But let me give you some help (if you need it) on numbers 8 and 9:

  9. a. Green, b. Blue, c. Red, d. Yellow

  10. a. Red, b. Green, c. Yellow, d. Blue

Body Language Awareness

"As long as we can smile at one another, laugh, embrace, hug, point and nod there's hope for a friendly future. The more I travel the globe making observations of the language of the human body, the more optimistic I become."
Desmond Morris, Anthropologist

Now that you've identified your personality strengths and have become aware of the things you would like to improve upon, let's move on and take a look at how body language can help you align and find balance in a parallel universe. Considering that ninety percent of all communication is non-verbal (or body language), its important to know how your body language expresses itself to others and how you can use this information to communicate more effectively.

The first time two people meet, they take notice. In micro-mini-seconds their subconscious minds are firing and sorting information. Viscerally sizing up the situation, they look for clues: What side is his hair is parted on? Is she looking straight into my eyes? How tense are his shoulders? How low is her neckline? How inviting is he? What colors does she wear and how is her energy?

Before a word is uttered, their body language has spilled the beans. There is a sense or level of comfort and trust. It is at that moment when the decision is made to fight or take flight. It's all about trust. Letting people know they can trust what you say and rely on your actions increases capacity for more "Yeses."

In each of us there is a desire to be loved, understood, recognized and valued for what we contribute to the world. This is what we want to express to the people we come in contact with each day. We want them to know how we can be of service to them and they can be of service to us.

This is not about judging or becoming critical of the way someone dresses or uses their body. Preconceived ego notions, culture, background or maybe past lives can get in your way of true understanding. I want you to be objective, to shift your mind to neutral and be open to whatever comes along.

Imagine hiking in the exotic Amazon Rain Forest. You travel through dense foliage, trudge through cold mountain streams, then come to rest near a Spathodea Campanulata. This plant is loaded with seed pods surrounded by small red flowers. Do you say, "Yee gauds, what possessed you to choose that color? What are those fuzzy horny things hanging from your center anyway? And that stem of yours has just got to go. Of course you don't. You accept the nature of it, the way it is.

I am asking you to accept the beauty and unique nature of each individual you meet, just the way they are and just the way they are evolving. I have put together a description of the body language of the various personality styles to help you distinguish what a person is saying and how you can respond in the conversation. Before you begin, ask yourself:

- What particular color style is that person?

- How does the person move his or her body?

- How has this person set up his or her environment?

The worst part about body language is that, for the most part, it is an unconscious action. The best part about body language is that, for the most part, it is an unconscious action. The good news is: you have a brain and you can choose at anytime to *consciously* use your body in different ways, therefore obtaining different results.

Color Communication

The following explanations are not etched in stone but are meant as some simple guidelines on your journey to obtaining "Yes."

Blue

Engaging a Blue is easy (for another Blue). The first thing you will notice about a Blue is an unsparing use of an infectious smile. The atmosphere of a Blue's world (home, cubicle, purse or clothing) is about attracting relationships. Virtually, everything they do is about building relationships. Family photos, brick-a-brac, memory builders and that alluring candy dish are dead giveaways. This comforting, comfortable energy puts you at ease and allows intimate expression and time to heal.

The body language of Blues is what neuro-linguistic programming experts describe as "approachable." Relaxed body, with one foot in front of the other, head slightly tilted, hands face upward and elbows away from the body. Their body sometimes can be described as a "door hinge," with the body turning to one side or the other to leave every possibility open.

A powerful way to connect with Blue body language is to mirror their behavior. (In other words, do what they do.) If Blue is a foreign language to you, take a moment to practice Blue language skills in the mirror. Try smiling, stand with one foot in front of the other, with your arms away from the body. Swing your arms loosely and imagine your happiest, warmest memory. Begin your sentences with a collective "We," "us" or "together," to appear inclusive and approachable.

The Blue personality's ability to nurture, connect with others and feel compassion serves them well as a healer. These qualities are the heart of healing. They open the door for a deeper, more rewarding life.

Health Note:

Blues need to stay in contact with people, so they can practice their light-hearted nature of service and good will. Relationships keep us healthy and grounded; they teach us so much about ourselves. It is vital that we have healthy relationships. However, Blues can become attached to destructive/hurtful relationships that are detrimental to their health and well-being. If this is the case, lose them. This is where you decide what kind of relationships you want in your life. It is never too late to have great relationships with family, friends and co-workers.

Green

Straightforward, analytical and time-conscious are the attributes you will recognize in the Green's environment. Greens don't mind clutter if it's their clutter and don't mind time wasted if they waste it. It's all about making the most of time.

A few family photos, an inspirational quote, their Coca Cola collection arranged around a gigantic coffee mug (saves trips to the coffee machine), the LIST and a well-placed clock on the wall will clue you into this project-oriented Green environment.

Greens' body language is straight forward, feet planted firmly on the ground and a level chin. They can appear stoic or unconcerned, which is most likely not their true attitude. Their shoulders are level, feet together and would prefer that you come right to the point. Prepare to have a great short conversation and always bring your list of facts. This puts them at ease, lets them know you are honoring their time and speaking their language. Once you have a sense that you have connected and have got their attention, you can if you like ask discretionary questions about the weather, family or pet. This will let them know you appreciate them professionally and personally. Starting your sentences with "I" adds authority and validity to the conversation.

The Green personality's capacity to identify, prioritize and finish a project is a valuable tool in being an effective self healer. It takes stick-to-it-ness and a sense of time-urgency to take charge of your life and heal whatever needs to be healed.

Health Note:

Greens tend to get stressed when they take projects and life too seriously. Seeing as how everything is a project, the challenge has to be how to stop fretting over past, present and future projects. The attitudes of *I'm right, I know better* or *Just get out of the way I can do it better by myself* can cause other people to step away from the counter and let the

Green with the sharp knife do the carving. These Green actions and behaviors lead to overload and big-time burnout. A preventive measure is to ask yourself: what is important my health and well-being, or the need to finish this project on time? How much time is my good health worth to me?

Red

Reds like clean, straight lines in black and white, with Red all over them. Their competitive nature is displayed throughout their environment with vibrant colors, trophies and awards. These trophies are benchmarks for reaching their next great goal.

Direct, credible body language identifies this straight shooter. Credible body language with the feet planted straight on the floor, a level chin and head-to-head conversations let you know they mean business. Red body language lets people know that you have a goal and you are going to reach it. By mirroring their language you honor their style and thereby obtain a huge advantage toward reaching your own goals.

The straightforward aggressiveness of a Red is a valuable characteristic to help you heal yourself and others. With this attitude you cut through the red tape of life and get right to the chase. In the process you gain confidence so you can reach new, loftier goals.

Health Note:

When there is confusion or delays in getting things done, Reds become stressed out. They can get angry and frustrated, or seem bullish. There is a tendency for them to beat themselves up and feel they have missed the mark. But this only leads to a bruised heart, which and can literally draw the life right out of them. Using your Red style to reach your goal can be done the hard way or the peaceful way, it is all about your choice of thought.

Yellow

You can locate WYELO, 97.5 just a little left of center on your radio dial. This can be said of a Yellow's body language. "Quirky, fun, fast-moving, frolicking" describes their cubicle, home, car etc. It feels as if a party is going to break out at any time. Yet they are equally at home lazing around their favorite hammock or charging ahead on a white water raft. This is the way Yellows would ideally express themselves, if the world didn't take itself so seriously.

Yellows' body language is very, very approachable. With abandonment and flair their elbows flap from their sides. If one foot hits the floor, the other must be dancing. With their chin up and their body rocking from side to side, they'll put a fun spin on everything.

This infectious energy can be too much for some folks. If you've ever had the urge to swat a Yellow fly then you know what I mean. But take a little time in front of a mirror to get into the energy of Yellow. Find your natural rhythm by bouncing your body as you stay in one place. Now kick it up a notch, until you are in the Yellow Zone. Practice this until you feel lighter and can smile at yourself. Now when you meet with a Yellow, you will have the advantage of honoring them by speaking in their language.

The Yellow personality has a powerful influence on your ability to be a healer. Your ability to expand your imagination beyond material or subjective matter opens your mind to the invisible power or energy where all things are possible. Visiting your Yellow Zone provides insight into the depth of your being and the cosmic world around you.

Health Note:

Keep in mind the Yellow style can kill you as well as cure you. The fun seeking Yellow has to regulate to the environment in which they live. This can mean taking a job in a project-oriented box or being forced to set goals and lists. This is how a Yellow can become stressed out or clinically depressed. They may turn to alcohol, drugs or food to ease their dis-ease, therefore with destructive results. Herein lies the decision to numb up or lighten up in your own Yellow Zone.

Suggested Words for Connecting

By combining what you have just learned about body language and the use of the following words, you will have an advantage when you approach and want to connect most effectively with other styles. The following key words are suggestions to help you engage in a meaningful conversation with the different styles.

Relationship Blue:

Connect with the Blue style using words like: *we, us, together, they, touch, feelings, details, connected, kindred, friendship, close, liaison, rapport, empathize, linked, collaborate, consensus, alliance, cognate, easy, peaceful, happy, understand, laugh, smile, hugs.* Start your sentences with *we or they or us or them* as connecting words.

Project Green:

Connect with the Green style using words like: *you, I, time, order, lists, skillful, expert, adept, special ability, knowledgeable, accurate, self-reliant, efficient, independent, unlike, studied, completion time, sensitive, deeply moved, introverted thinkers, private people.* Start your sentence with "Do you have a moment?" Or, "I want your expert opinion on…" Or, "Let me explain the order."

Goal Red:

Connect with Reds using Red-style words like: *I, you, results, purpose, target, aim, ambition, end, time, intention, destination, stop, goal, objective, motivation, reason, committed, driving force, deliberate, strong, tenacious, consciously, knowingly, willingly, calculate, concentrated, acute.* Start your sentence with an authoritarian "I" or "you." After all you are the authority.

Fun Yellow:

Connect with the Yellow style with words like: *you, we, fun, play, recreational, merry, good time, blast, frolic, ball, laughs, high time, pastime, hobby, engage, wow, enthrall, hospitable, party, accommodate, treat, joke, chocolate, colorful, spellbound, charm, fascinate, mesmerize and razzle-dazzle.* Start your sentences with "This will be fun," or "You are so good with ideas, how would you…?"

Getting a Grip on Fear And Doubt

Reed Hasting's first job was a math teacher for the Peace Corps in Swaziland, Africa. After graduate school, he started his first company, called Pure Software. The company was later purchased for a pile of money, reportedly three-quarters of a billion dollars. And this gave him the money to be able to start Netflix, a DVD mail order business, which earned $688 million in revenues in 2005. When asked about being a CEO he replied, "I struggled as the CEO of the first company. I had my doubts and I worried whether I was doing the right thing, most of the time." When asked about how he felt today, he said, "Now with Netflix I still have doubts and worries, but I control them better."

It's presumed that once people have reached a pinnacle of success, they exude confidence; doubt rolls off of them like so much melted butter on a basted duck. What Reed Hasting is saying is that success can be measured by the control you have over fears and doubts.

If you feel as though you are diagonally parked in a parallel universe, you may want to examine what emotional thoughts or attachments you have acquired over your span of life that are keeping you from "Yes!" It's not easy to change one's life. I know all too well the commitment and determination it takes. Yet, I am asking you to become deeply—more deeply than ever before—aware of how life has evolved and is changing for you. There is only one thing standing in the way of your success.

" 'Tisn't life that matters!
'Tis the courage you bring to it."

Sir Hugh Walpole

Five Things You Can Do
to Control Fear And Doubt

⚙ 1. Confirm And Declare What You Really Want

You say to yourself, "I want a new car," and the first thing you know, the radiator on your present car blows a gasket. Then you (unconsciously) decide that cars are too much of a hassle so you buy a bus ticket. "Hassle" is another way of saying: I'm afraid I won't make the right choice. I doubt my ability and will probably buy a lemon and end up paying for repairs till the cows come home. Or maybe you think you don't deserve a new car. Remember the Universe only knows one word, "YES." It says "Yes" to fears and doubts as accurately and proficiently as it will to your order for a new car.

Make a firm decision about what you want and confirm it with your heart and gut. Ask yourself is this what I really want? Declare it to yourself to increase your determination and commitment. Share this information with others only when you are sure of yourself.

⚙ 2. Visualize "Squeezing" Possibility out of Every Moment

There is nothing in the entire world more powerful than your mind and its ability to visualize and hold a dream to its fruition. The seeds of all things material were first germinated in the fertile mind of man, in collaboration with Universal Law.

Sit in a quiet place where you will be undisturbed. Listen to your thoughts. Let them ramble on here and there. Let your imagination run wild; let it stretch as far as it can to the far reaches of the galaxy and back again. Now ask yourself, what is it that I want? "Squeeze" on possibilities by asking what would make your life more fun, more interesting, more meaningful?

Allow what you want to come to mind. Let go of any doubt or fear that may be standing in the way of your saying "Yes!" and accepting it. See it getting clearer and more pronounced in your mind. What is it like to smell, taste, hear and touch your dream? If you feel you're not a visual person, ask yourself, "What will it feel like to touch my dream?" You have the power to tour life through your vision.

3. Meditate on The Unfolding of Your Dream

Most people think of meditation as something you do to calm your body and release your mind of all thoughts. They are right. However, besides being a great stress reliever it is the place where you can literally sense your dreams unfold.

Take time to breathe and relax into the silence and nothingness of the moment, right where you are right now. This is where nothing is required of you. You don't owe anyone anything. Your time is yours to do with what you want. The same is true of your dream. It is yours to do with as you wish. Let your body, mind and Spirit breathe into your dreams. Let go of fear and doubt and let universal, unconditional love fill your every pore. Appreciate the connectedness and beauty of every living thing and how this loving energy that surrounds your dreams enhances the world.

"To hold and nurture a dream is to affirm all that is possible."

4. Accept Eagerness to Learn And Willingness to Change

Some people are going to be in total agreement with the changes you are making in your life, while others are going to look at you as if you've lost several vital screws to the door that is flapping in the wind.

- "There is something about you that's different."

- "It's changing our relationship and I don't like it."

- "I want things to be the way they were."

It is here that you can begin to doubt your commitment and let your determination waver. Fear and doubt will cripple your efforts and even squash your dream or vision. It is a matter of being aware of the small voice that is saying: never mind, my life is fine just the way it is, I don't want to rock the boat and upset people. Once you are aware of this voice, this old behavior that has not let you experience "Yes!" you can do something about it. You can decide at that moment not to listen and to do what your heart knows is good for you.

It used to be that I would awake every morning with the intention of exercising. Within seconds of that thought, a list of excuses would emerge from my mind and an hour later I opened my eyes again. Sound familiar?

My willingness to change was being impeded by old habits and behavior. I was listening and wanting to follow my old patterns and expecting different results. Nothing changed until I became aware of those voices, then thanked them for sharing, and got up and did what I needed to do anyway.

"Some people will, some people won't... so what."

⚘ 5. Creative Action to Stir Up The Universe

If you've been waiting to get over your fear before you take action and express your true self, don't bother. There is nothing in the world worth doing that isn't going to scare you. Fear is the natural companion of creative action.

One of the ways I have found effective for taming my fears and doubts is to take action in the direction of my dream or vision.

Let's say I want the experience of a new kitchen. I have no visible funds to support my dream; I only have my vision of what I think it should look like. I spend time imagining where the appliances might go, the color of the floors, cabinets, light fixtures and tile.

It's all in my head at this point. It's then that I do what I call "stirring up the Universe." I make one little move toward my dream. Maybe I arrange a vase of flowers and place them in the window, buy a cute rug to cover the hole in the floor or I go so far as to talk to a cabinet maker and find out what my dream will cost. It is not necessarily the size of the action as it is the intention of the action. With intention behind your actions, the Universal energy, the God Source, or Ki Energy of life supports you and what you want from life.

You are standing in the crossroad of your life. To move forward and say "YES!" to life, you must give up self-limiting fears and put your trust in the Spirit within you. It is the only way to truly become the balanced, authentic, true self communicator you desire to be.

A Word of Warning!

None of the ideas presented in this chapter is going to help unless you are willing to take this next vital step. If you want to make lasting and permanent changes in your life you have to be prepared to devote time and energy to your life. This is your time, time for you. It is what your soul has been longing for. You deserve to experience the greatness that you are.

This requires a willingness to apply the information you have read and practice the *Ki Energy Exercises* daily and thereby become more and more conscious of the importance of the body-mind connection and how this connection will empower and heal you.

Resource Center

Here are additional resources for further reading:

- *What Color Is Your Personality?* by Carol Ritgerger gives different insights into why knowing your personality style is important.

- *Working Woman's Communication Survival Guide* by Ruth Herrman is another good source for understanding and implementing personality style information.

"Know your personality dimensions and know the strengths and weaknesses of the people around you. They won't seem nearly as difficult to work with."

- *The Color Code: A New Way to See Yourself, Your Relationships and Life*, by Dr Taylor Hartman

"Personality is that core of thoughts and feelings inside you that tells you how to conduct yourself."

꧁ ꧁ ꧁

The following are three websites that enhance the topics covered in this chapter:

www.sciencedaily.com

www.sciencecareers.sciencemag.org

www.haleonline.com

Ki Exercise # 3

Pour yourself a cup of your favorite tea and sit comfortably in your chair. Take a deep breath and let your body and mind relax. Take the cup of tea in both hands. Feel it warm your hands. Breathe in the aroma, let the steamy vapors touch your cheeks and nose. Observe the color and bouquet. Slowly with devoted thought, take a sip, swish it around in your mouth, and let it permeate your being. Relax into the silence.

Make your body comfortable. Straighten your spine, rest your shoulders and curl up your tail bone. This aligns you to the energy of the earth and heavens that move through your body, strengthening your resolve and assisting you in reaching your highest potential. As you are one with your warm cup of tea, you are one with yourself. Just as you are one with yourself, you are one with all people. Feel your connectedness, your oneness. Gently set your cup down.

Sit with your palms facing up and focus on the warm sensation in your hands. Your hands hold healing energy. Your hands are an extension of your heart. Your hands, heart and mind will heal your body. Close your eyes and focus your attention on the part of your body that is experiencing an ache or pain. Send loving, healing energy to that area.

You are using Ki Energy right now. Right now you are one with the Universal Spirit. As you focus on loving, healing thoughts, there is no room for worry, fear or doubt. Breathe in, breathe out. Take a deep breath and tell yourself, "Today is a great day and I am ready to accept my goodness."

Chapter 4

Okay, So What *Is* the Speed of Dark?

"Be bold. If you're going to make an error make it a doozy and don't be afraid to hit the ball."

Billie Jean King

Courage is usually thought of as a moment in time when a person jumps, crashes or charges into the dark unknown to save the day. For some, courage is the U.S. Army Lance Corporal, who walks the streets of Iraq or Afghanistan, knowing full well the possibility of pandemonium or even death that waits. For others, it's the teenager who steps in front of a moving bus to rescue a child. Or the courageous, homeless mother of three who struggles to find work, food and shelter. Courage is all of these things, and more. However there is another type of courage I want to talk about here, one that you may have overlooked or deemed insignificant.

I think it's important that we talk about this particular kind of courage, because without this essential element, the rest of the information on these pages is utterly and completely useless. The type of courage I'm referring to will help you get through everyday challenges or crises. It will help you lose weight, get a better job, increase your prosperity flow, help you deal with the loss of a loved one—and much more. You may not have regarded this as courageous. Yet it takes courage to grow up to be who you really are. It takes a specific type of courage to know what you want, be willing to pay the price, and experience the pain and discomfort it takes to change old habits and behaviors.

"Get a backbone, find your gumption, and use your will power," echoes down the halls of guilt and rattles up the corridors of woulda-shoulda. These slices of wisdom are playing and rewinding just before your adamant Monday morning declaration: "I'm going on a diet!" And, I might add, just after you find yourself swathed in chocolate by noon.

"Here I go again. What happened to my willpower? I'm a miserable failure." This is like cycling on a gerbil's wheel. You go round and round and get absolutely nowhere fast. It's great to get motivated or charged up about losing weight or increasing your income, but when you hit the peak and run out of steam, it's like a drunk waking up in a sleazy hotel without a memory. You not only feel guilty, you have no idea how you got there or why you feel so lousy. At that point there are only two choices: keep trying or give up.

The Only Part of Life You Can Control Is Inside You

Most of us give up on ourselves: "Why bother? I'll just have to accept my fat body or slim bank account." After all, it's just not worth feeling guilty about. This obviously eats at self-esteem and, over time, creates an empty cavern where your backbone once existed. If you believe the problem to be too many fatty foods, too much take-out, too much sugar or dairy etc, too little respect at work, too little income or too many bills, think about it. This is *so* not the problem. All these things are outside of you. The only part of life you have any control over is inside you. The only way you can change life is from the inside out. And by the way, giving up is not a solution.

"You have the ability to do anything you choose to do, follow through and complete it."

Ann White

Believe yourself to be courageous. I want you to take this word COURAGE and stuff it deep in your heart of hearts and believe you are courageous clear down to your bones. When you have embedded this belief into your psychic you will be free and truly be willing to say "YES!" to life. Sue Patton the author of *The Courage to be Yourself* defines courage this way: "Courage is the ability to do what needs to be done, or feel what needs to be felt, in spite of fear."

When I was diagnosed with cancer and said, "No" to chemotherapy, I felt a door slammed shut on a chapter of my life. I found myself in a pitch-black corridor leading God-knows-where. I was left without a clue as to where to go, who to trust or what to do next. The only thing I had to follow was my inner Spirit and voice. With fear and trepidation, I investigated naturopathic physicians, holistic remedies, wacky theories and a few oddball treatments. I read labels in dark and dingy health food stores where I assumed you had to wear Birkenstocks and never shave your legs. Staggering and falling at times in the darkness of the unknown was part of the journey. But I had to wonder …what is the speed of dark? How soon will I be healed?

At The Speed of YOU

How fast will any of us go through the darkness of a personal challenge or crisis? The answer is: the speed of YOU. Whatever your internal-speedometer permits is the appropriate speed. Past experiences, cultural beliefs, your set of standards and your physical condition will be determinants in how courageously you step up and face what needs your attention. However, understand that it is not how fast you go, but the lessons you learn along the way. The fact is, that lesson you are learning is always teaching you how to be more courageous. If nothing else, it is showing you what you *don't* want, so you will step up and express your true self—and can then have what you really want.

Some people are not willing to accept what happens in life as a lesson. They would rather believe that things just "happen" to them, things over which they have no control. This makes it easy to justify, rationalize and defend the right to stay stuck, blaming others and never confronting one's personal habits or behaviors.

Many people live stuck lives. They get stuck sideways emotionally, physically and spiritually in a life of mundane survival. All they want to do is to get through their life—like the little worm—unscathed, with as little pain as possible. But their theory is wrong; life simply doesn't work that way.

Harriet Jones is an intelligent, attractive, fifty-something, sideways-stuck woman. For over fourteen years, she has sidestepped the necessity of confronting her estranged husband about a divorce. Instead of going back to school and advancing her education so she can support herself, she takes low-level, dead-end jobs. There was the time her neighbor arrogantly built a fence straight through the flower bed on her property; she was nice and said nothing. Harriet knows what the right and just thing to do would be. Yet she doesn't want to endure the consequences of risking a jump into the darkness of the unknown to confront life head on. There is no question that her physical ailments (arthritis, high blood pressure and insomnia), reflect directly on her sideways style of living and her inability to move forward.

> *"The spirit, the will to win, and the will to excel*
> *are the things that endure. These qualities are*
> *so much more important than the events that occur."*
> Vince Lombardi

We all face trials and calamities in life—divorce, a death in the family, career changes, personal injury or any other human circumstances that are painful and leave scars. We all know what it's like to feel as if you are left in some dark, unknown place. Yet in this darkness or void is *Spirit*, the *Holy Spirit*, if you like, which is the internal part of you that will never leave you. When you go within and began to connect and trust the energy and power of the invisible source, courage grows and becomes second nature.

Unlike the popular belief that courage is only bestowed upon a privileged few, everyone possesses courage. I like the way David R. Hawkins, M.D., Ph.D., author of *Power vs. Force*, defines courage:

> "Courage implies the willingness to try new things and deal with the changes and challenges of life. At this level of empowerment, one is able to cope with and effectively handle the opportunities of life. For instance the energy to learn a new job skill is available. Growth and education become attainable goals. There's a capacity to face fears and character defects and to grow despite them; anxiety also does not cripple endeavor as it would at lower stages of evolution."

You have this kind of courage. It is already within you. All you need to do is exercise your courage muscle. In the previous chapters, you've become aware of the power and presence of your unique personality style and how these various characteristics integrate, enhance and support you. The following exercise will help you establish a base line for your personal level of courage and this will allow you to build up your determination and resolve for when you need it the most. The exercise will give you a better idea of the areas you will want to work on as you develop a courage-building plan.

Are You A Person of Courage?

Take a deep breath and let it out. Read the following questions and circle the numbers one through ten, as they describe your level of courage, with one being *least applicable* to you, and ten being the *most appropriate* description of your courage.

1. I stand up for what is right, even if I stand alone.

   1 2 3 4 5 6 7 8 9 10

2. I don't cave in to negative peer pressure.

   1 2 3 4 5 6 7 8 9 10

3. Fear or failure doesn't prevent me from trying things.

   1 2 3 4 5 6 7 8 9 10

4. I am not afraid to express myself just because some people disapprove.

   1 2 3 4 5 6 7 8 9 10

5. Courage is something I am born with and can develop.

   1 2 3 4 5 6 7 8 9 10

6. Courage is important to the quality of my life.

   1 2 3 4 5 6 7 8 9 10

7. Evil will triumph as long as good people do nothing.

   1 2 3 4 5 6 7 8 9 10

8. I am not afraid to move forward even though I know there will be consequences.

   1 2 3 4 5 6 7 8 9 10

9. Fear and doubt hardly ever creep into my thoughts.

   1 2 3 4 5 6 7 8 9 10

10. I am not afraid to confront others when I believe it is the right thing to do.

    1 2 3 4 5 6 7 8 9 10

11. I face fears and character defects and grow despite them.

    1 2 3 4 5 6 7 8 9 10

12. I am not afraid to experience pain or discomfort if it means I will win.

    1 2 3 4 5 6 7 8 9 10

13. I am not afraid to fail because I know that every wrong attempt is another step forward.

    1 2 3 4 5 6 7 8 9 10

14. I take care of myself first and this is a courageous act.

    1 2 3 4 5 6 7 8 9 10

15. Within me is the power to achieve and succeed at whatever I am determined to do.

    1 2 3 4 5 6 7 8 9 10

Calculating Your Courage Baseline

Now let's take a look at your *Courage Baseline*. Understand that this is just a "baseline"—a starting point for you to work from and not a place for flinging wild judgments upon your ability to be courageous. Most people never take the time to determine their level of courage and therefore have no way of knowing what they are capable of. To determine how courageous you are, add up the numbers you have circled and decide from the chart below your baseline of courage.

135-150
Great Job!

96-135
Congratulations—
more to be revealed.

31-95
Give yourself a pat on the back
for loving yourself.

15-30
Additional counseling may be needed
to help you become more assertive.

A Plan to Increase
Your Determination And Courage

Formulating a plan to boost your level of determination and courage will help you to work through obstacles and barriers that keep you from experiencing "Yes!" Here are three fresh ideas and tangible practices you can incorporate in your daily lifestyle. Utilize each of these to cultivate your inner courage.

⚅ Prepare to Be Lucky

Not only are you responsible for your life, but for the amount of luck you develop in your life. Choosing to make the right move or decision at this moment puts you in the best place to receive your good luck for the next moment. Living a fortunate life, filled with possibilities and wonder, is not something that happens to only a few providential slobs who stepped on a precise blessed vortex at the exact right time.

"The more you prepare the luckier you appear."
Terry Josephson

Instead the fortunate life comes to those who are prepared to accept it. Preparation is a natural state in mother nature. A seed sprouts and grows into a giant Sequoia tree when placed in suitable surroundings. And the same is true that when you place yourself in the appropriate environment, there is no limit to what a human being such as you can accomplish.

Forget your age, gender, health condition, occupation, education or financial status. Forget that you are too short, too tall or have too many warts. This is all B.S. The only thing you need to concern yourself with is what you're doing to prepare yourself for success. What are you doing right now that is preparing you for your next great moment? Your whole life is one big state of preparation. Everything you have done in your life so far has prepared you for today's experiences.

Two essential things in the preparation for being lucky or successful:

- First is a willingness to ask for what you want, and
- Second is to stop worrying.

❧ Learn to Ask for What You Want

Asking for what you want sounds simple enough, but for those of us who have experienced the what-ifs, ya-buts, or can't-evens in this life, asking for what you want can seem like an ineffectual pipe dream. Yet the act of asking and declaring what you want is, fundamentally, the most powerful action you can take to counteract the sucking-in of negative thoughts and hindering beliefs.

Drinking in negative thoughts is poisonous. It's a slow-acting poison, but lethal nonetheless. Negative thoughts or words are powerfully toxic energy when you let them dictate your life. Your choice of thoughts, words and actions are what drives your life, so choose wisely.

For instance, when your doctor says you have six months, two years or ten years to live, ask yourself, "What do I believe?" Do you believe that in six months (or whatever) you will not be sitting here? You have the same choice when friends download their woes of the day, just to vent. They're not seeking sound advice or solutions, just dumping their unwanted negative, useless thoughts. Ask yourself: What is this energy doing to my mind, body and Spirit? How does it affect my ability to ask for what I want and to believe I can have it?

❧ No Room Here for Professional Worriers

There are people who worry as if it were a profession. They would literally be lost if they didn't have something to worry over. They worry about getting a job. When they get the job, they worry about keeping it. When they get promoted they worry about how proficient they are. When all those worries dissipate, they look for something new to come along to replace it. They do the same with their family, friends and pets. When asked not to worry, they'll look at you as if you'd invited them to jump off a sheer cliff, while assuring them that the tiny pillow below will catch their fall. Worrying is debilitating. There is no room in a "Yes!" life for worry.

> *"The greatest glory in living lies not in failing,*
> *but in rising every time we fall."*
>
> Nelson Mandela

❧ Don't Let Negativity Get in The Way

Negativity gets in the way of your dreams and aspirations. Yet it is never too late to ask for what you want and prepare to receive it by letting go of the negative energy that is around you. Every successful person has had to learn to deal with life's hurdles by working through negative thoughts and obstacles so they can accomplish his or her life's dream.

Her father was a Spanish professor and her mother was a failed writer who died young of "sheer misery." It seemed that Alice Adams was destined to share her mother's fate. At 16, she entered Radcliffe College, where a male professor told her to "forget about writing and go get married." After graduating Radcliffe, she worked briefly for a New York publisher, and then in 1946 she married a Harvard graduate and moved to Paris. "I loved Paris," she said, "except I disliked him so much."

In 1948, the couple moved to San Francisco. Unhappy and unfulfilled, Adams went to see a psychiatrist, who advised her to stop writing because it must be making her miserable. She did the next best thing; she divorced her husband in 1958 and supported herself and her son with secretarial work. "I kept writing," she said, "but it struck me as an excessively neurotic thing to do—to be wasting all that time on something I was not good at. Although, in some recesses of my mind," she added, "I must have thought I was good."

Through the grace, talent and the tenacity of her efforts (and I might add, the willingness to ask for what she wanted) that countered negative thoughts and worries, Adams escaped her mother's destiny. Against all odds, she continued to write. She courageously prepared herself for the life she wanted. Alice Adams was the author of *Careless Love*, *Superior Women*, *Southern Exposure*, and *After the War*.

⚅ The Magic Is in The Decision:

What does it take to motivate you? What has to happen before you go over the line and out of your comfort zone and into the magic of creating the life you truly want? In my case the threat of slowly dying of cancer without fulfilling my dreams forced me to make a decision that eventually led to a healthier, happier life. You don't have to have a wake-up call, as such. Diet, exercise and spiritual connectiveness will all help, but the main thing that's going to thrust you forward into your new life is the magic of decision.

> *"Decision is a risk rooted in the courage of being free."*
> Paul Tillich

Abracadabra, hocus-pocus, ala-ka-zam and, presto, it's magic. In this case there is no slight of hand or waving wand that transforms things. The kind of magic I am referring to is the shift in energy that occurs when a decision is made. You may have had the experience of deliberating and fussing over details and options for some period of time but once the decision was made everything fell into place and you found that all you really needed to do was decide.

Most people who are stuck lack confidence in their ability to make decisions. Confidence, like courage, is developed by making a small decision that leads you in the direction of bigger, more courageous decisions. Let's say you want to attend college. Plenty of preparation is needed to get your mind, body and soul ready for the journey. The small decision to apply for a scholarship can be a start. Decisions to purchase school supplies, arrange transportation or housing may, by themselves, seem inconsequential, however each choice shapes and encourages your next decision, until before you know it you're writing your last term paper.

People often put off making decisions because it can seem gargantuan. Yet it's the little decision that opens doors and builds confidence in crafting the "Yes!" life. Stop waiting for a guaranteed outcome. You'll end up making no decision at all—and that, in itself, is a decision.

The Reverend Theodore Hesburgh, former President of the University of Notre Dame, said about decisions. "My basic principle is that you don't make decisions because they are easy, you don't make them because they are cheap, you don't make them because they are popular; you make them because they are right."

This kind of decision making can be uncomfortable. In fact, I guarantee you will be uncomfortable. Moreover, if you are not uncomfortable you haven't stretched far enough. Stay with your discomfort; you'll realize that there is no choice but to do what is right for you and the people around you.

Two years of limbo, Kathy had tried every way to find a job. Part of the problem was just that: she was *trying* to find a job. This self-proclaimed "interview queen" had schlepped her resumé hither and yawn with exhausting results. "You're too diversified," "You're over-qualified," and "You want how much?" All of this was true. Kathy's skills included carpentry, electrical contracting, computer savvy, writing and teaching. Her real passion was seminar development, but that just seemed too narrow a field, and probably out of her reach. She had a lot of talents, but like most people who are unemployed for a long period of time, her confidence waned and her focus wobbled.

Kathy is a Yellow with a Blue streak. Her creativity, approachability and emotional way of thinking dominate her personality. Her linear thinking of Red and Green had taken a back seat and were nearly nonexistent. However, after some self-examination she realized she would have to make some adjustments in order to get the kind of job she wanted. She'd been going about this using her emotions and intuition. Now she realized that she needed to balance her approach.

In a prescreening phone interview, listening attentively, linear thinking met intuitive thinking. Her qualifications were right on the money. The job was exactly what she was looking for. Now to cinch the job, it was a matter of listening for the clues as to what the employer needed. When the screener, in passing, mentioned a portfolio to demonstrate her talents, light bulbs came on. It had never occurred to her to build a portfolio that would showcase her abilities.

Hanging up, she immediately started writing. She focused her time and energy into getting her ideas down on paper. In other words, she turned on her Green brain and made a list. How could she be of service to the company? The interview was one week away and she was determined to give it her all, not matter what. Taking a deep breath before the interview she checked herself: Do I have enough facts or am I too emotional? Do I have too much emotion and not enough facts? Am I thinking with both my emotional and rational mind, and is this the best decision for me? Kathy did get her dream job when she decided to—and because she decided to.

⚙ Persistently Believe, to The Extreme:

The definitive driving force of courage is persistence—extreme persistence. So many people, including me, have at one time or another, given up, given in or walked away when success was right around the corner. We've said to ourselves, "Well, that didn't work," brushed our hands of it and moved on to the next thing.

It may have been because of what other people have said or simply a lack of self-confidence. It is depressing to know you could have had what you wanted if you had just kept on trying. This giving up is a coward's way out and since you have given up coward-hood for the

"Yes!" life, you'll want to be more persistent.

We have, within each of us, the ability to achieve great things if we are willing to go the extra mile, move out of that damn comfort zone and push ourselves until it hurts.

The point is, persistency perpetuates momentum and so once you believe in your extreme dreams, the momentum is set. What you have wanted to achieve comes to you easily. Prepare by asking for what you want, make a magic decision and go for it. All the while, believe to the extreme that you can have it, then let go and let it happen.

I love reading the obituaries. It makes me realize how fortunate I am to be alive. It's also a great place for inspiration and insight into people's lives. When I ran across Morris "Moe" Levine's story I felt I had to share it, not simply because it's a story of determination, but because it demonstrates a willingness to dream no matter what the circumstances.

"Moe," as his friends called him, was a sales representative for a major manufacturing company. He had a passion for football. When the local paper announced that the Dallas Cowboys were having tryouts in his neighborhood, Moe became ecstatic. Dreaming of being a place-kicker, he set out to prepare himself by practicing every evening at the local park. The day of the tryouts came and Moe found himself waiting on the goal line with all of the other hopefuls.

He stood there squinting through thick lenses in dark, tortoise-shell-rimmed glasses. His graying hair coiled around a Macintosh hat that capped his five-foot-four height. Is it any wonder his friends and family thought him foolish when, at the age of fifty-nine, he announced his decision?

He was not selected that year. But after the tryouts, Moe proudly said, "I kicked the ball through the goal post at twenty yards," then added, "I pulled every muscle in my body doing so." Now this is where Moe could have—and some say should have—given up. But you see, he had a dream, and nothing was going to stop him from experiencing this dream at what ever level he could. For the next ten years, Moe tried out for every major league team in the United States and Canada.

Now you might say this was an unproductive thing to do, but was it? Doesn't it speak volumes about the act of persistence? Doesn't it make you wonder whether it is right to put limitations on a dream just because it seems outrageous? On the walls in Moe's office were framed rejection notices from every major league football team. There also hung an official document from the Dallas Cowboys making him an honorary place kicker.

> *"Facing fear directly and with courage, I discover my true strength and power."*
>
> Albert White

My Plan for Building Courage And Determination

❊ What do I want to ask for? What is my dream?

_____

_____

❊ What steps will I take to prepare myself for a terrific outcome?

_____

_____

❊ What decision do I need to make in order to move forward?

_____

_____

❊ Who do I need to forgive—myself or another person—to free my mind of negative thoughts and allow more "Yes!" into my life?

_____

_____

❦ What habits do I want to incorporate into my life that will bring me more balance and peace?

_____

_____

❦ Here is a list of the things I like most about the people in my life. How do my friends, family, co-workers etc. influence my life style?

_____

_____

A Story of Courage

"I, too, have had cancer," she sighed, "I was told a year ago I only had a couple of months to live and to get my affairs in order." As she swiped her dark, silky locks from her eyes, her solemn lips broke into a tiny smile, "And I'm still here," she added.

That was my introduction to Myrna Franklin as she greeted me after a speaking engagement.

You could describe Myrna as a torn spirit, a downtrodden, apparent victim whose mind, body and soul had been horrendously and insidiously raped—for that is what happened. But when you get to know Myrna's true Spirit, you realize this is not the core of who she is.

Sexually abused as a child, then married into an abusive relationship, Myrna spent over thirty-five years of her life witnessing and experiencing satanic ritual abuse in a spiritually based cult. Although she felt raped in body, mind and spirit, she didn't let it stop her from holding to a dream deep within her.

One day a decision was made; a decision to follow her dream. Before she could fulfill her dream she had to clear the way so she decided to go within and lovingly search for her true self. She found a beautiful little girl, who needed desperately to be loved, parented,

92

believed in, cuddled and listened to. She spent time with this child. She played with her, laughed with her and let her know how adorable, loveable and special she really is.

Myrna had said "Yes!" to life. Yet the decision to go for her dream entailed letting go of old beliefs and established support systems. In fact, virtually her entire emotional support structure collapsed. Her family, friends and career were all in some way or another connected to the cult, subsequently she found herself disconnecting from everything she had known to find a new life. She was starting over, completely from scratch. "I felt as if I were in a dark hole with no way out."

I asked Myrna what helped her get through this tough time. "God draws me along to himself—guiding and directing me, answering my prayers. I had no idea whatsoever of what was up ahead for me. Yet I was able to stay on track, focused, and balanced because of the supportive and loving energy that helped me tenaciously and persistently fight for my dream."

Today Myrna is a domestic abuse counselor. Happily married and full of life and love she gives back to others what knowledge she has gained from her life experiences.

Defining Courage

What is the definition of courage? For me, courage is more than simply a physical action. It is a state of mind as much as a state of body—it is in this context that I write. As a keynote speaker, or workshop leader, when I share my experience of overcoming cancer without chemotherapy treatment, I am often asked what kind of courage it takes to turn away from one life and design a new one.

This decision is not made from a desire to be courageous, but with the realization that life is too painful the way it is. When there is no other choice but to move on to hopefully something better, something better always comes to you when you let go of the past.

Resource Center

An excellent book for further studies:

▓ *The Courage to Be Yourself: Woman's Guide to Growing Beyond Emotional Dependence,* by Sue Patton Thoele

---

Ki Exercise # 4

Set your favorite cup of tea by your chair and take a deep breath. Now let it out. Let your entire body relax into a pool of your former self. Continue to breathe deeply and continue to relax.

Close your eyes for a moment and let your mind follow these words to your courageous center. Within you, at your core, is an internally and eternally courageous soul. It is the goodness of you that instinctively knows what is right for you. It guides you. It gives you the courage to follow your dreams. Take time to be with yourself. Appreciate how much you are truly loved, cherished and supported.

Breathe in and let it go. Place your hands on your abdomen, a couple of inches below your bellybutton. This is the center of your body. Tighten as hard as you can and hold the abdominal muscles under your hand for the count of thirty. Focus on your muscles and the slight burn you feel. Continue to practice this each day, working your way up to one hundred and more seconds. This exercise deepens your ability to connect with your body and mind and simultaneously will strengthen your determination to express courageous acts of love.

Take another deep, deep breath and let your mind, body and soul come alive. Refreshed and renewed, you are ready to say "Yes!" and "Thank you so much, no matter what," to a brand new day.

Chapter 5

All Aboard the "Yes!" Train

"Love is a fruit in season at all times,
and within reach of every hand."

Mother Teresa

No Baggage Required

Are you ready for the ride of your life? Are you ready to live your life waking up every morning saying "Yes!" to the world? Are you ready to move out of the doldrums of the ordinary life and into the extraordinary life God has meant for you? If the answer is "Yes!"— which it had better be by now—there is something more you will need to know.

In the first few chapters, you explored characteristics of individual personality styles and began to recognize the importance of balancing these characteristics to create more *harmony* and *oneness* in your life. This oneness, this self-love, this sense of universal love and respect for all humanity is vital to your health, well-being and willingness to say "Yes!" to life. Without an awareness and deep appreciation of your oneness, it is nearly impossible to love and respect yourself and others.

Then in the previous chapter, you determined your level of courage and discovered how this powerful element will help you move forward and overcome the dark unknowns of life. These elements are fundamental and they lay the groundwork for the kind of life you so desire. There is, however, one more essential component you must undertake in order to board the "Yes!" Train.

But Before You Board...

You bought your "Yes!" Train ticket the day you were born. And although you've been loitering around the station for years, gathering baggage, waiting for the right moment, now it's time to board, to drop your old ways, and begin the ride of your life.

However, there is one question you must answer before you board the "Yes!" Train: When you're going on a trip, do you pack your dirty clothes, the contents of your junk drawer (everybody has one) and the kitchen sink? C'mon now...yes or no?

Of course not! Nobody wants to lug around stinky, unusable, heavy stuff. I think we'd all agree with that. But stop for a minute and consider the excess baggage you may be carrying right now. Think about all that useless heavy stuff that's dragging you down: resentment, frustration, worry, anguish or bitterness. Most people are burdened in one way or another by heavy baggage of this sort.

The fact is, they've overpacked for the trip of their life. They're weighted down with unnecessary negatives and have not yet discovered the power and importance of forgiveness. They suffer from headaches, stomach aches or backaches. They closely scan the drug commercials for symptoms of the next great disease. They wonder why their relationships are guarded or disintegrating or why they don't have a career they really enjoy.

Dragging around pounds and pounds of excess baggage wears a person out. There is nothing that will improve your health, wealth and relationships more than dumping it immediately. And the best way to do this is to practice the act of **forgiveness.** It's a known fact that forgiveness will help you lighten your load and with your newfound freedom from that extra baggage, you'll have more fun. You need to learn to travel light!

Five Good Reasons
to Lighten Your Load And Travel Light

✺ Lose your baggage and gain your balance.

Hoping to advance your career, you've spent hours preparing for a company presentation. Your speech is polished and you have the attention of your audience. You are just about to make your point, when out of nowhere you see a carrot. A *carrot*?

In a nanosecond, your mind wanders off to the time you were imprisoned in the carrot factory. Old memories come flooding back. You freeze. You swore you would never face another carrot as long as you live. Thrown off balance, you find your focus becoming cloudy and your confidence waning. What happened here? There is no logical reason for your reaction, yet there you are, carrot scared.

> *"Forgiveness is giving up the possibility of a better past."*
> Carma Brown

Of course *you're* not afraid of carrots, so this story may seem, at first, irrelevant. But I invite you to fill in the blank with your own paralyzing memories and emotions—the ones that keep *you* from living fully. Unwittingly we all accumulate and drag around stuff that can get in the way of moving forward and, in doing so, actually stunt our spiritual and mental growth. It's so easy to be drawn off balance by old negative thoughts and emotions that get in the way of our goals and dreams.

✺ No more baggage, no more abuse.

Maybe you know someone who believes; "The cops have their radar gun pointed directly at me," or "It's not my fault the light turned red," or maybe, "Defensive driving is my personal war game." The Universal Spirit of God and the law of attraction always say "Yes." So when you believe you are the victim of circumstances and don't let go

97

of the emotion behind the thought, you will continue to draw to you the consciousness of being victimized.

> *"To forgive is to set a prisoner free and*
> *discover the prisoner is YOU."*
>
> Unknown

Did you know that it is nearly impossible to be pushed around and feel victimized when you lighten your load by forgiving yourself and others of past indiscretion? Everything you were carrying around seems so much lighter and you gain phenomenal energy that liberates negative emotions. It can be the turning point towards unconditional love and the ability to see your pain and problems as opportunities for growth.

People who have not yet learned to let go of hurtful and resentful memories have a tendency to feel that everyone is picking on them or is out to get them. Forgiveness opens your heart; you no longer feel the need to defend yourself or fight off the advances of imaginary enemies. Your relationships become authentic, honest and caring. There is true relief from anxiety, fear and doubt, as well as a deeper sense of oneness with yourself and others.

✂ Travel lighter and you'll travel healthier and happier.

Forgiveness can lighten your load and give you a tremendous breakthrough in your pursuit for improved health. Sometimes it only takes a suggestion that will lead you in the right direction.

"You probably won't do this," assumed Dr. René Espy N.D., D.C. "but, I recommend you listen for thirty days and nights to this cassette tape by Louise L. Hay on *Healing Cancer.*"

Three months of homeopathic treatments had slowly improved my overall condition; my hair was no longer falling out due to low thyroid, my color had returned to my grayish skin and I had gained some weight. Nevertheless my body had hit a plateau. It was time to shift gears and explore another avenue of healing—*the power of the mind.*

Dr. Espy's words, "You probably won't do this," struck a cord. She was on to me! If you want me to do something, just try and tell me I can't or won't. Faithfully, night and day, I listened to the tape. I began to peel back layer after layer of deeply embedded resentments, mostly directed toward my mother. The frustrating feeling of helplessness and hopelessness that had tightly wound themselves, like a wild wisteria vine around my heart and soul, began to loosen.

Within two weeks there was a surprisingly noticeable difference, so much so that Dr. René commented on my progress by asking what I had been doing differently.

"All disease comes from a state of un-forgiveness."
Louise Hay

Forgiving saved my life. It was at this turning point I realized I would be practicing the art of forgiveness the rest of my life. While non-forgiveness doesn't cause cancer or disease, it's creates the proper environment—the "growing medium"—that permits disease to develop. Until this experience, I never realized how deeply held emotions affect health and the integrity of life. Nor did I have a clue as to how this false thinking could be corrected so easily.

Clean it out—and find "Yes!" money.

Everyone has a hall closet. I don't know about your hall closet but if it's anything like mine, it's full of stuff. One old glove, a half a can of dried shoe polish and a size two t-shirt that never fit, with the motto, "Don't Eat Yellow Snow," blazoned across the front. Now that's *stuff*! Stuff I never used and never will use. Yet there it is, crawling out to greet me every time I open the door.

It's true that every material thing in your life is a reflection of your thoughts and actions. Let's say you have a cluttered closet. I lay odds you also have a cluttered mind, full of stuff you don't need and will never use again. This can manifest itself in your life in various ways.

For instance, think about your bank account or your checkbook. Do you know your balance? Do you have an abundance of funds so that your needs and wants are easily paid for? Do you conduct business openly, caringly and lovingly? Is there stuff cluttering up your life and preventing you from reaching your financial goals?

Travel tip: "It's better to bring half of what you think you need and twice as much money."

Lee Roy Brown

A surefire way to increase your bank account is to clean your "mind closet"—and it wouldn't hurt to clean out that hall closet as well. Physically and mentally moving stuff around, letting go of what is not needed, changes the energy surrounding it. This stirs up the Universe and makes space for new and exciting possibilities.

Lighten Up And You Won't Need A Moving Van

You may think I'm kidding, but I'm not. If you continue to accumulate the crappy stuff that so far has run your life, by the time you've reached your "golden years" they won't seem so golden. You will need a moving van, entourage or a wheel chair just to haul around your sorry bags of stuff.

"If we practice an eye for an eye and a tooth for a tooth, soon the whole world will be blind and toothless."

Mahatma Gandhi

Letting go of agonizing, unresolved problems rooted in the past is essential to your health, your effectiveness as a communicator and ability to stay focused in the present. It may also be one of the determinants as to whether, years from now, you will be healthy and mobile.

Diseases such as arthritis, heart disease, cancer, and diabetes are becoming commonplace in our society and not just among elderly people. ***It doesn't have to be that way at all!*** Take into consideration the correlation between a particular disease and a strongly held belief. Consider for a moment the connection between the disease and forgiveness:

- **Arthritis:** Critical of self and others. Feels unloved and harbors resentment. Feels victimized and blames others.

- **Heart Disease:** Lacks joy in life and thereby exhibits a "hardening of the heart" plus longstanding stress and strain.

- **Cancer:** Feels deep-rooted hurt and resentment that silently eats away at the self. Harbors feelings of "what's the use?"

- **Diabetes:** Longs for what might have been and finds no sweetness left to life. Feels a deep sense of sorrow and a need to control.

These are brief descriptions of the underlying thoughts of a few common diseases. To learn more about the correlation between thought and "*dis*-ease" in the body, I recommend that you read the book, *You Can Heal Your Life* by Louise Hay, Hay House Publishing.

Other Benefits of Forgiveness

Forgiveness research is a relatively new and uncharted field. Prior to 1985, only a handful of studies had been completed and in the fourteen years since, fewer than sixty more. Nevertheless, social scientists have begun to quantify the power of forgiveness in a variety of subjects:

Health: Studies show that letting go of anger and resentment can reduce the severity of heart disease and in some cases, even prolong the lives of cancer patients." G.A. Pettitt, MA, MSE has written an article at www.iloveulove.com in which he states: "The forgiveness process has a very specific definition. It means the process of canceling the conditions in you which block the flow of love and goodwill towards yourself or another, independently of the actions of anyone else. It can also be defined as a healing of memories."

Crime: A study conducted in 1995 by the University of Montgomery analyzed how much the desire for revenge (the opposite of forgiveness) factors into the committing of a crime. The study clearly indicates that forgiveness education could play a key role in reducing the vengeful responses that lead to criminal acts.

Relationships: Family therapists have successfully used forgiveness as a tool to reconcile couples when other techniques have proven ineffective.

Other areas of research include studies of the power of forgiveness in at-risk adolescents, Vietnam veterans, substance abusers, terminally ill and elderly patients, victims of domestic violence, HIV/AIDS patients, and many others.

> *"Forgiveness is both a decision and a real change in emotional experience. That change in emotions is related to better mental and physical health."*
>
> Everett L. Worthington, Jr. Ph.D.
> Campaign Executive Director of *"A Campaign for Forgiveness"* Research

Your Forgiveness Baseline

Forgiveness is a healing journey for both body and soul. You may know in your heart that you want or need to forgive someone, yet the course toward peace and ease can be difficult.

To move forward, it often helps to have an accurate sense of where you are right now. The following exercise establishes a forgiveness baseline, and includes two parts: *State of Your Life* and *A Situation And A Specific Person*. It will help you assess your thoughts, feelings and behaviors, as well as the relationship between the condition of your life and your level of forgiveness of a specific person. You may find that simply following this exercise moves you forward toward inner peace.

Part I: State of Your Life

Take a moment to contemplate these questions, and then write a brief explanation of how you feel and how you would like it to be different.

1. What is the condition of your health?

_____

_____

2. How well do you like your work?

_____

_____

3. How is your love life?

_____

_____

4. What is your financial situation?

_____

_____

5. How well are you organized?

_____

_____

6. What is the condition of your relationships with friends and family?

_____

_____

7. What is the condition of your checkbook?

_____

_____

Part II: A Situation and Specific Person

This exercise contains two sections and its purpose is to allow you to assess your level of forgiveness. Bring to mind a specific person toward whom you want to measure your level of forgiveness. Rate each item as to the degree to which the thoughts, feelings and behaviors match your own.

Person's Name: _____

How do the following statements match your feelings about this person and situation? Choose a number from 1 to 5, with the number 1 indicating that you Strongly Disagree and 5 that you Strongly Agree with the statement.

Strongly Disagree (1) ———————➤ (5) Strongly Agree

1. I feel angry when I think about him or her.

      1   2   3   4   5

2. I'm going to get even.

      1   2   3   4   5

3. I replay the offense in my mind, dwelling on it.

      1   2   3   4   5

4. I'll make him (or her) pay.

      1   2   3   4   5

5. I live as if this person doesn't exist or has never existed.

      1   2   3   4   5

6. I keep as much distance between us as possible.

      1   2   3   4   5

Adding up the points my score is _____

Now assess your Forgiveness Actions toward this person using the same rating scale:

Strongly Disagree (1) ⟶ (5) Strongly Agree

1. I prayed for this person and asked God to forgive him or her.

    1   2   3   4   5

2. I clearly see this person's good points.

    1   2   3   4   5

3. I looked at the source of the problem and tried to correct it.

    1   2   3   4   5

4. My resentment is gone.

    1   2   3   4   5

5. I took steps to resolve the rift: wrote, called, showed concern.

    1   2   3   4   5

6. I feel peaceful.

    1   2   3   4   5

Adding up the points my score is ⎯⎯⎯⎯⎯⎯

This is not a test where the highest score wins. Rather, it is an opportunity to weigh your resentment and anger against your compassion and willingness to forgive. If your score on the first part is higher than your score on the second part, it's time ask a few insightful questions:

- Do I really need to hold on to resentful, angry feelings?

- Is this situation affecting my health and the way I communicate with others?

- How do I feel about the person now?

- What can I do to let go of negative, harmful emotions?

The Colors and Forgiveness

This may help you to understand how some personality styles hold on to their resentments and negative feelings. You'll also learn some suggestions for releasing them.

Relationship Blue

Blues are sensitive and deeply hurt by broken trusts and dishonest relationships. If they feel powerless and are unable, for whatever reason, to express their feelings, they have a tendency to repress the memory until it eats away at their self-esteem and health.

To Release: Crying helps. There is nothing better than a good cry, but after that, take time to separate your emotions from the deed and don't take the offender's actions personally. Recognize and let go of negative, harmful thoughts immediately by speaking up and telling the other person how you truly feel. This is where you practice courage as well as forgiveness.

Project Green

The loss of control, the wanting to be right and feelings of confusion haunt the thoughts of the project-oriented Green personality. It is hard for Greens to move on and enjoy their sense of purpose when they're harboring ill will or resenting past indiscretions. These emotions stop the ease of movement and restrict the flow of love to Greens.

To Release: Take yourself on as your own project. Make a list of the things that are bugging you and tie them to the negative emotion you want to release. When you are aware of how ill-serving these emotions are to your well-being, your logical mind will quickly let go and open the channels to your genius once again. You may want to add a little Yellow just for the fun of it.

Goal Red

Anything that instigates a loss of control or gets in the way of Red's targeted goal will infuriate and frustrate. If Reds feel constricted, so do their arteries—and so do the people in their life. Losing their patience, blowing up on the outside also causes Reds to blow up inside.

To Release: Stress and strain are not a necessary by-product of reaching your intended goal. Incorporate your Blue and Yellow personality traits and allow your diplomatic side to understand where someone is coming from and your carefree-freeform thinking mind to release your tension.

Fun Yellow

When Yellow's fun and creative genius is hampered with the struggles of the world, they edge their way toward the nearest addiction. Comforted by drugs, food, sex or some other escape they lose touch with their Spirit and their artistic flair.

To Release: To strengthen your ability to let go of old hurtful perceptions, incorporate a few Green personality qualities. Make a list. List the people or things that have hurt. Now using your creative abilities, draw a picture of how you feel. Express your healing through your art. Incorporate your Blue personality and to get in touch with the emotional energy you want to express.

These are just a few suggestions to help in the process of releasing old, negative, stagnant thoughts.

The B.S. of Forgiveness

Just in case I haven't made a strong enough argument for the power and importance of forgiveness—and in case you still have a few excuses—I want to make it perfectly clear: *non-forgiving is B.S.*—as in, BOGUSLY STUPID.

⚘ B.S. #1

If I forgive, I'll have to trust the other person and I am afraid I'll be hurt again. Trust has nothing to do with forgiveness. In reality, trust and forgiveness are very separate things. To forgive is to free yourself from an uncomfortable emotion, nothing more. You're just accepting the fact that the other person is a fallible human being—one who must earn your trust.

⚘ B.S. #2

To forgive is a sign of weakness. Nothing could be further from the truth. The forgiving person is strong enough to be assertive and is able to express his or her feelings directly, rather than lying or dissembling. It is a sign of character that most people truly respect.

> *"The weak can never forgive.*
> *Forgiveness is the attribute of the strong."*
> Mahatma Gandhi

- Thomas Takashi Tanemori, with the Silkworm Peace Institute, is a Hiroshima A-Bomb survivor. He came to America in 1956 as an embittered teenager, trying to contain his anger and seek revenge on the American people. "My life, since I was eight years old, has been a long struggle to understand the demise of my home town, the confiscation of my childhood, and the horrible indignity of a bomb attack that marked the beginning of the Nuclear Age. It has led me to finding peace in my heart, and becoming a man of peace." He felt marooned by a dark and bitter past and wrestled with the persistent ghosts of history, learning what it means to be a minority. Then he experienced his own inner spiritual transformation and discovered the importance and power of healing the human heart by turning from revenge to forgiveness.

❦ B.S. #3

By forgiving I will be letting the offending party get away with something. The assertive act of forgiving brings to the forefront the wrong that was done and makes clear that it will be unacceptable in the future. It helps you understand and stand under what you believe to be true. You always have the option of choosing not to forgive—or becoming more aggressive yourself, if the other person repeats the offense again and again. But then again what's in it for you?

❦ B.S. #4

I can't forgive until I forget. Good luck with that one! You'll forget a wrong number sooner than you will forget an offense. You don't want to carry this stuff around so the faster you let go of the emotional charge attached to it the better. Forgetting is often the results of forgiving.

- When his father was killed by two ex-convict hitch-hikers in 1985, John Gray endured the devastating event with tremendous grief. He decided to use his pain as a challenge to himself. He set out to help those who wronged him. In 1986, Dr. John Gray, author of the popular relationship books, *Men are From Mars, Women are From Venus*, formed a team of teachers and counselors to teach the power of forgiveness to a group of prisoners in San Quentin. It was an experience that brought about release that was overwhelming for the prisoners and for the teachers, including Gray.

❦ B.S. #5

It's phony to act forgiving if I really don't feel it. We often empower ourselves to do uncomfortable things by acting as we have already done so. We do this because we know this is in our best interest.

- **Step One:** Go through the motions of forgiveness and your emotions will catch up.

- **Step Two:** Forget about living a life of separation—you are Spirit and, in Spirit, there is only one source for all things.

∞ B.S. #6

It's not fair, I shouldn't be the one. "Forgiveness is more difficult for the people who have a strong sense of narcissistic entitlement," according to Roy Baumeister of Florida State University. People with a high sense of entitlement appear to see forgiving as risky and unfair, particularly if they have not received any sort of amends or apology from their perpetrator. Face it: life is not fair and not about you. Be easy on yourself, take care of yourself by realizing that holding on to these emotions will not do your body or your mind a bit of good.

- Nelson Mandela, a South African activist and statesman, was elected in 1994 to be the first black president of South Africa. He was born in Umtata. In 1944, Mandela joined the African National Congress, a civil rights group promoting the interests of black Africans. However, in 1962 he was sentenced to five years in prison for his activism. In 1964, he was further sentenced to life imprisonment, convicted of sabotage and treason. Mandela soon became a worldwide symbol of resistance to apartheid, South Africa's rigid segregation policy. He once said, "If you want to make peace with your enemy, you have to work with your enemy. Then he becomes your partner."

Time to Drop Your Bags

"It is not easy to find happiness in ourselves, and it is not possible to find it elsewhere."

Agnes Repplier

You have to remember that you cannot change anyone. You can only change yourself. But remember: you "create" the other person by your actions and intent. Resentments and hate are the obstacles that keep many people from clearing up their unfinished emotional business and achieving harmony with others. Having the courage to go beyond fears opens the way to forgiveness of those who have wronged you. It releases a love that can make you psychologically immune and increases your chances of survival under all conditions.

Our sanity and well-being require us to stop being obsessed by past events or misunderstandings that threaten to destroy our present happiness. Our fixation on such problems may exacerbate their gnawing control over our emotions. There comes a moment when we need to say "Enough already!"

The following are various techniques I have used over the years to sort out my thoughts and learn to forgive myself and others. I've suggested these to some of my clients who have hopped on board the "Yes!" Train. Try them out for yourself:

Five Techniques for Forgiveness

1. Take a walk and do the talk. The Red Bluffs of the Sacramento River have a well-worn path along the water's edge where, as a child, I would walk and tell my problems to the water. Walking opens the body, frees the mind and makes right the soul. And water is a great listener and a great healer. Nowadays, I visit the Pacific Ocean; it listens and send my thoughts out to sea with each wave.

2. Bury the grudge—literally. On a piece of paper, write out the thing you are angry and frustrated about. Jot down all your feelings and emotions that are stuck in your craw. Bury it all in a pot of soil. Decide that for three months, you'll act as if you've forgiven the other person. Then dig up the paper, review your feelings and decide whether you want to make your forgiveness permanent.

3. Write an unsent letter. Write a letter to the other person but don't send it. Express fully how you feel, why that person's actions have hurt you and made you angry. Let yourself get as angry as you need to. Then declare assertively to yourself that you forgive them. It may take several days and many drafts to get the letter just right. You've completed the exercise only when you feel that the letter you've written is so honest and authentic that you would welcome receiving it yourself. And actually sending it is always an option for the future.

4. Enlist encouraging help. Have a friend or relative take the role of the other person. Confess all your anger and painful thoughts to that person. Encourage the "stand in" to resist your attempts to rationalize your past behavior or any excuses you might dredge up. Remember to use the word "I feel" or "I am" when addressing the problem. Discuss only the way that will lead to forgiveness.

5. Be thankfully sorry. Use a deep breathing exercise to achieve a fully relaxed state. In your next breath, say to yourself, "Thank you, God," and "I'm sorry." Thank you, God, for the opportunity to grow through this experience. I am sorry for anything that I may have done, intentionally or unintentionally, to attract this into my life. Sit with these words for awhile and through your thankfulness you will find peace.

Summing It Up

Don't live in the past; you will get buried alive there.

All families, to some extent, are dysfunctional. They didn't get that way overnight. It took many generations of dysfunctional behavior to perfect the strongly held dysfunctional beliefs we've acquired today. Beliefs such as insecurity, separatism, hatred, violence, war, scarcity and poverty continue to leave their mark on us today.

Poachers, bootleggers, thieves and a grandfather who deserted my mother's family when she was five are but a few of my dysfunctional ancestors. The history of these people was never an open topic for discussion around our kitchen table. It was like the pink elephant in the corner—if we don't speak of it, it's not there. Nonetheless, these haunting ghosts lurked in the shadows of my parents' words; "What makes you think? ..." or "You'll never get ahead..." "Don't get your heart set on it." "Life is hard." "Don't rock the boat." Or "Remember there are only two spots on the football team and hundreds of guys trying out."

Samuel King, the grandfather I never met, inadvertently left his legacy. Given that I've had a blessed life, I can hardly imagine the hardships my mother must have endured. Growing up during the great depression, she learned how to scrounge for meals, was shamed by divorce, and quit school to support her family and grew up without her father. Insecurity piled on insecurity, resentment upon resentment resulted in a heritage steeped in distrust—a legacy which my mother passed on to her family.

A new inheritance was created the day I had compassion, understanding and forgiveness for my mother, father, and Samuel. I realized our oneness. His blood not only runs through my veins, but—good and bad—his actions have shaped my life in ways I will never fully know. This may seem like forgiveness taken to the extreme but, trust me, this kind of forgiveness is well worth the effort.

Resource Center

✻ *Forgiveness, The Greatest Gift of All* by Gerald Jampolsky, provides great insight into why forgiveness is a gift to be used and nurtured. "*The symptoms of suffering and pain have their roots in our unforgiving thoughts...*"

✻ *You Can Heal Your Life* by Louise Hay. Louise played a significant role in helping to heal my body and therefore change my life.

✻ *The Course in Miracles* opened my mind to the power and value of nothingness.

Ki Exercise # 5

Take a deep cleansing breath and let it out. Find a comfortable place to be alone and take time for yourself. Breathe in another deep breath and as you exhale, allow all the tension to leave your body. Slowly become aware of letting your scalp, forehead and face relax. Focus your mind on your body as you let your tongue, throat and shoulders release. Let the feeling of relaxation pour over you—down your back, in and through your abdomen and down your legs to the tips of your feet.

Notice the change in your body since you began to let go. Notice how tense your body is right now. Now let it relax even further... there is nothing you need hold on to. If you are holding this tension with your body you are also holding it with your mind.

Now, breathe in, breathe out and say to yourself, "Everyone makes mistakes. I forgive the person I have held hard in my heart. I forgive myself for any past mistakes."

Breathe in and breathe out. Check your body with your mind. Do you feel pain or discomfort anywhere in your body? Instead of shifting your position, focus your mind energy on the painful area and let your mind soothe your body. Repeat these words:

"I love myself for who I am right now and who I am
becoming. I release all tension. I let go of all anger
and resentment. I let go... I let go... I am at peace."

Close your eyes. Clasp your hands together and stretch them above your head. Completely stretch your body. Relax. Stretch again to allow the peaceful, centering energy within to fill you.

Chapter 6

Giving It Up to "Yes!"

"The strongest principle of growth lies in human choice."
George Eliot

Everything I've shared with you in the previous chapters has been intended to help you become the healer of your life; through healthy communication and by learning to use the potent light of Love. You've learned about personality styles and how to use this information to your advantage. You've gained knowledge of your inner courage and the power of forgiveness has helped you clear away old fears and limitations. I have shared with you how I overcame disease by connecting with the divine intelligence of the body, mind and Soul. This leads to healthy communications with your true self and thereby healthy communications with the world around you. Each of these is an essential component to saying "Yes!" to your life.

However there is even a greater essential element that *must* be practiced for you to become the healing communicator in your life.

The Word Is "Surrender"

Surrender may seem like an antiquated word with overtones of war and sacrifice, but nonetheless it is a powerful and essential part of saying "Yes!" and living a life of opulent peace. Resistance to giving up and relinquishing a belief or object is normal human behavior. No one wants to let go of the familiar. The dictionary defines *surrender* as: To stop fighting because you are unable to win, to give up possession of something, to give up control and give up to authorities.

Definitions of Surrender

Let's examine these definitions of surrender to enable you to understand how they relate to interpersonal communication and healing.

To stop fighting because you are unable to win. It is the Red personality style that believes in the need to fight against something they consider bad. They can be heard saying, "I'm going to fight my cancer" or "I'm fighting for my job, life or very existence." Did you ever notice that when you fight against a problem you exacerbate the problem? Whatever you focus on, you attract to you, so the harder you fight against it the bigger the perceived enemy. Give up the fight and direct your focus on the unquestionable power and presence within. Let this be your beacon, let this lead you *to* and not *against* healing.

To give up possession of something. The truth is you own nothing. You came into this world with nothing. Plain and simple you'll go out of this world with nothing. However, our Blue personality wants to hold on; it identifies and attaches feelings to relationship with people, places and things. If someone or something is lost to us we try to hold on to it in various ways. However, tightening your grip will strangle the life of anything. Take a good look at what really matters in your life. You will find that the only thing that matters is the Love you have for yourself and for others. Let go of the materialistic, egoistic way of living and begin living from you heart. Let your heart be filled with Love and you will know what really matters.

To give up control. One of the hardest things to do is to loosen the grip you have on controlling of your life. This is a Green personality style challenge. The Green is so attuned to managing life as a project that letting go means not know what the outcome will be and that is distressing. Relinquishing control means giving up the way it has always been and trying something different. Observe what you are resisting. Ask yourself only one question. Is my set of beliefs and perceptions about this situation working for me? If the answer is yes then keep on doing it the tried and true way. If not step away from the counter, let the higher power within you take the controls. You will have a much safer and interesting landing.

To give up to authorities. Give up! Hands in the air! Read 'em their rights! Okay, sorry I've been watching too much Law and Order. All color personality styles have a tendency to give themselves over to doctors, lawyers, nurses, chefs, and anyone else who claims to be an authority. Particularly, Yellows who may be having too much fun to be distracted with trifle matters such as a checkbook, relationship or health issue. They would just as soon hand it off to an authority to fix. Remember you are the only authority on your life. No one, anywhere knows more about you than you. There is only one authority to give yourself to and that is the highest authority, the source of all things, God or Spirit. The only thing required of you is to trust this higher authority and let it guide you to whatever is needed.

Five Different Ways to Surrender

There are various degrees of surrender. Everyone journeys down the path of life with their own inclinations, preferences and velocity. No two people are on the same path. Some are unaware that there is a path while others are afraid there is. It doesn't matter how aware or conscious you are it is only a matter of time before you will encounter surrender. Here is a list of approaches people have taken when surrendering:

1. Right Turn Clyde:

This is when you clearly look at a situation and immediately shift gears and head in another direction. This surrender is relatively easy. There is very little trepidation or fear of the future and limitations are ignored or pushed aside. It just becomes obvious that this is the next thing you should do and you do it.

Sharon Houseman was on her way out of the Aquatic Center when a flier at the front desk caught her eye. It was a sheet of paper enlisting volunteers for the Forest Chapter Memory Walk, a local fund raiser to prevent Alzheimer's disease.

Sharon looked the information over and automatically began to think about how she could contribute. Never mind that she walks only with crutches, the result of an automobile accident that led to the amputation of half of her left leg two years earlier. The Alzheimer's cause was dear to her heart and she was determined to do her part.

"I had been wondering what I was going to with myself," she said. "I wanted to give, but how? Then it occurred to me, I can do this," she recalled. "I can't walk, but I decided to swim instead." So swim she did. Sharon found sponsors and completed 44 laps one Friday morning and raised $400. It was a typical gesture from a woman who's anything but typical.

Sharon's life took a drastic turn on April 30th 1996, when her Toyota collided with a semi trailer north of Seattle. The entire left side of her body was weakened by the trauma of the impact. She spent four months in the hospital.

She also lost her memory, giving her insight into what life is like for an Alzheimer's patient. When she returned home she couldn't remember the layout of the house; it took strength and courage and a certain amount of surrender to come back. She couldn't remember where her bedroom was but she knew she had a rose garden. Eventually, most of her memory returned. "There are things I can't remember, but I don't worry about it," she said, and then added, "I just do the things I *can* remember."

Sharon's life was forever altered by the accident, but not diminished. Her determination to help others in need presses on uninterrupted. She teaches English as a second language, volunteers at the Interfaith Caregivers Association and the other constant in Sharon's life is swimming, three days a week.

2. Friendly Poke'n Folks:

A friend or someone close to you sits you down and tells you the truth. You may not want to hear it, but because he or she is speaking the truth from the heart, you are willing to open your mind to the idea of changing some behavior. You know the truth—it resonates deep within, there is no denying it. It may take some time before you take action but, know this, it will eat at your soul until you do.

Phone: Ring-a-ding-ding

You: Hi Charlotte, how are you doing?

Charlotte: Blah! Blah! Blah! Problem, problem, problem.

You: Oh, really, not any better hey?

Charlotte: Blah, Blah, Blah problem, problem, problem.

You: Charlotte, you've been saying you were going to do something for quite some time…

Charlotte Yabut, Blah, Blah, Blah, problem, problem.

You: Well, because we are dear friends and you know I only want the best for you. You know that I am telling the truth when I say you have to do something about this. This problem is harming your relationships, health and happiness. I don't want to see you continue down this path day after day with no solution in sight. You need to make some changes, you need to face facts and decide to do what is good for you. I know it's hard to hear this and the way to recovery may be hard too but I am here for you. I support you. I love you. However you have to make the decision to do what your heart tells you to do.

Charlotte: Blah, blah, blah… Thank you.

3. Graceful Ganders of A Grateful Welcome:

There comes a moment of surrender after you've shucked and jived around something you've desired for a very long time. You've exhausted every probable and plausible opportunity, you've prayed and cajoled. You've done everything you know how to do, everything that is yours to do. It is then that you have a choice to stay in the present story of limitation or give up and appreciate the life you have right in front of you. The moment you began to appreciate and surrender to grace, you opened the door and allowed God Spirit to give you what you need. My dear friend, Reverend Mary Midkiff, of Woodland Chapel Religious Science Church, in Salem, Oregon, wanted a child desperately. She shares her story of surrender:

"I was already attending a Religious Science Church so I was a pretty positive person; however, I had never tried getting pregnant before; I had always tried *not to*. I figured it would happen quickly because my mom had ten kids and I had always been very regular, healthy and easy about my periods. I just figured all that stuff really worked well. So it was a shock when it became a problem.

"It became obvious after a year that is wasn't going to happen "naturally." My husband Lynn and I had started going to a fertility specialist and doing different procedures. Some were painful. For the first time I began to doubt my body (it was determined right away that the "fault" was mine). After taking hormones for a while and getting pregnant, it was devastating when I had my first miscarriage. I was assured that a first miscarriage was common but second miscarriages weren't. So having a second miscarriage was much, much worse. At first I grieved, especially about the miscarriages. Because it's physical, it takes a lot to recover from a miscarriage. Your body is hurting and hormonal and you feel like you've lost a "real" infant, but have nothing to bury or mourn.

"We pursued adoption through a couple of agencies. We were willing to take an older child or a child from another country. But it looked pretty impossible anyway. It was either going to be way too expensive or take so long that I would be too old under some guidelines. An arranged adoption opportunity came up through my church. I thought it was the perfect answer, like a divine demonstration. It would happen soon, be inexpensive and just right for everyone.

"When that didn't happen I felt worse than I had for the miscarriages, because I had been so sure that it was the answer. I fell apart and cried in despair, but only for about thirty minutes. I know that sounds strange, but it's true. Very quickly I realized that God was somehow in all this and I had to accept that. I also realized how hard it would be for a mother to give up her child.

"Frustration and a feeling of unfairness hung over me. I felt it was unfair to say there are so many children needing homes and "you can always adopt", because it certainly didn't look that way to me. But there was some part of me that said, 'This is so frustrating, it's weird. I don't usually get this frustrated about things. It must mean that I'm supposed to have my own naturally.' But I never really said that out loud, and went through a lot of painful moments.

"I decided I just had to move on. The nursery became a storage room and eventually I closed the door on it. I got into Practitioner training and studying the Science of Mind principles, because I felt so strongly that I was supposed to and thought I'd stopped trying to a have baby. But I never really did. Everything I learned in class I applied to getting pregnant. With each new technique, concept or author, I felt I was grabbing it by the throat and demanding: 'Okay, how are you going to help me get pregnant?'

"Bit by bit, I worked through things, surrendering at different levels all the time. There were many turning points. The "final" turning point was one day when Lynn and I were out walking with the dogs. We were talking about them, as usual, as if they were our kids. It suddenly broke over me that if these two dogs were the only children I ever had, I would be fine. It was more important to love, regardless of what the object of that love was. And I know I loved them. It was an incredible feeling of peace, release and acceptance. Two weeks later I conceived my daughter."

People often ask if a person has to "bottom out" in order to let go and surrender to a higher Spirit? I suppose in a way the answer is yes, but it's like that old saying, "It's always in the last place you look." It's the "last" place you look because once you find it, you stop looking! So once you surrender, things start turning around and you can see that spot as "the bottom" because it was the lowest you went. But the bottom doesn't have to be as bad as it sounds. It's all up to how well you listen to the Universe and respond. "Whatever you say, God, I will do."

> "The Universe whispers first. If it has to,
> it will eventually have a house fall on you."
> Oprah Winfrey

4. Draw A Line in The Sand:

Enough is enough. There comes a time when a line of demarcation is drawn in the sand and you decide to say "Yes!" to life and try something different. You don't know how, why or who, however at that moment, you have surrendered to the still, small voice within you that already knows all that stuff. Your God Spirit was just waiting for you to say "Yes!" so that everything needed to heal the situation could fall into place. Mary Ann Fanyak of Salem, Oregon shared her experience of drawing a line in the sand and deciding enough is enough.

"In 1986 I was diagnosed with what the doctors called a movement disorder closely resembling Parkinson's disease and Multiple Sclerosis. This insidious unpredictable disease of the central nervous system gradually develops symptoms of fatigue, stiffness, spasticity, brain fog, and eventually, in my case, uncontrollable flailing. Over time it became increasingly difficult to do the things that I enjoyed.

"I was in incredibly bad shape by the time I went to dinner with a few friends after church one Sunday. I couldn't sit still long enough to sit at the table. People on each side of me had to hold me down so I wouldn't slide out of my chair. Because I was moving so radically and uncontrollably I was also perspiring profusely. My weight had dropped to one hundred six pounds because I was constantly moving. Even at night I would fall out of bed because I couldn't control the flailing.

"This was the turning point. This was it. I couldn't do this anymore. I had no inner resources left. I had tried and tried; I'd done everything I could, but had to stop there. I told myself I would do whatever it took, but I had run out of ideas. I'd have to let go and let God show me the next thing to do. This was my way of saying, literally, 'Yes!' to God.

"It was apparent to me that I had to do something. I had to try something. I left the restaurant that day with a sense of resignation and surrender. I turned to my minister, and said, 'I have got to do something about this now.' Within days my dear friends formed a prayer circle; they too felt the urgency that something had to be done now.

"I had remembered watching a segment on the television program 60 Minutes about an operation or procedure that was suppose to help PD. I couldn't remember much more about it but it did give me hope that something could help me. The funny thing was that from the moment of my decision to do something I kept running into people, places and things giving more information about this procedure.

"The following Tuesday I kept a scheduled an appointment with a local neurologist. After the two hour drive up and down the I-5 corridor from Salem to OHSU (Oregon Health and Science University) in Portland for many years I welcomed the chance to meet with a specialist close to home.

"However, the day before my visit, the doctor' s office received a phone call from a nurse at OHSU who said, 'I was cleaning out some cabinets here and I ran across a request for Mary Ann Fanyak's records. I don't know if you are aware of this program we are offering called Deep Brain Stimulation but I think she would be a good candidate for the program.'

"My neurologist went on to explain a few details of the procedure and that they only had two open spots left in the program. Ironically, it was the same procedure I'd heard about on television. It was clear to me that God was saying, 'Please, please don't hesitate. *Wake up* and take this gift.' From that moment on nothing was ever the same again!

"The consultation with the OHSU surgeon gave no guarantees and made clear the risks of brain surgery. He went on to say that they may be able to improve a few symptoms but things like speech should not be expected. I relayed this to my minister, who responded, 'That's ridiculous! I *refuse* to accept that and I hold the truth of you. Your speech is going to be perfect.'

"The surgeon did, however, make me feel I was in experienced hands. I jokingly called him the master chef. He asked me, 'If we can eliminate one symptom what would it be?'

"I replied, 'The flailing.'

"Within weeks I had been evaluated and scheduled for an

8:30 AM surgery. The pre-surgery spiel about no food or water was addressed. In preparation, a stainless steel cage resembling a soldier's helmet was secured to my scalp by boring small holes; it prevented any movement. Then the word came that the surgery had been delayed and that another doctor would be performing the surgery. I was unhappy about that but what could I do? I surrendered once more.

"However as time wore on, I became downright nasty. I was thirsty, no water. I was hungry, no food. Believe me, sucking on a wet tissue does not cut it. I couldn't do anything but lie there and wait. By my description, I was a basket case. To look at me, you would have thought I was calm and composed, but I was raging inside. I just wanted them to do this and get me out of there!

"The only thing that helped keep my sanity was the presence of my daughter, Jennifer. She stayed right with me throughout many a long day and especially long nights. The presence of my husband, Mendi, and the constant phone calls from both my sons, Doug and Sean, were wonderful and helped me to stay positive.

"Finally, the word came down and I was wheeled into the operating room at 8:30 p.m, twelve hours later. It was then the sawing began. I was purposely kept conscious so they could detect problems, however they used an electric saw that I swear came from 1100 BC. I'll never forget that sound and the vibrating of my skull and ears. Again I had to let go and let God.

"Suddenly I felt a hot liquid flowing out of me; 'Oh my God I'm bleeding!'

"My sense of things told me something was wrong. I grabbed the nurse's hand and asked, 'Am I going to die? I need to know the truth, am I going to die?'

"Calmly she replied, 'No you are not going to die, but we do have a problem.'

"Well, the problem was that the doctor had mis-measured the entry points by a substantial amount and had severed an artery. Inside I was questioning: this is my head, what were you people thinking? I didn't know where this was all going but almost anything was better than what I had been dealing with all those years.

"I had been keeping my eyes closed throughout this whole thing so I could focus. I opened my eyes and who should I see but the master surgeon I had previously consulted with. I was wondering what this guy was doing just standing there. He was preparing to walk out when I said loudly, 'Come over here!'

"As he came closer I went on, 'Why weren't you here when this happened?' Later I thought about suing, but the energy around such an act was not worth it to me.

"He explained that he was a couple of doors down with an emergency procedure. He watched as the acting surgeon tied off the artery and hoped for the best. The surgery continued as they implanted two small electrodes in my brain and fished a wire down my neck and chest to a small box under my skin near the stomach area.

"A week later, they inserted batteries into the box and hooked it up. The change was immediate. It was like someone had literally turned on a switch. The shaking, the tremors and the flailing had disappeared. I was able to walk normally and my speech is near perfect.

"Only a month earlier I was headed for a wheel chair and a nursing home. I felt as if I were doomed to watching my own slow and steady and inevitable decline. My expectations weren't very high. I didn't know whether this would fix it or even help.

But there was a rage burning through my body and I was just sick and tired of being sick and tired. I knew that whatever I had to do I had to do. I accepted this knowing it was in God's hands and he always says yes to my will and intention.

"These days I go for walks by myself; something I couldn't do before. I recently completed a 3K walk for the Multiple Sclerosis Association. I feel so blessed. Before this affliction I was a radio personality and communicating was terribly important to me. For years I had struggled to let people know the person that was inside me. I'm reminded of the words to a song, 'Freedom is just another word for nothing left to lose.' I feel I've traveled the path to freedom and now its time to rest and play. It is my privilege to share my story with associations and groups who need to remember the power of saying 'Yes!' to their lives. It wasn't easy but it was worth the price of surrender."

5. Go to The Window:

There's a bit of dialogue from the 1976 movie, *Network*, that really speaks to me:

"So I want all of you to get up out of your chairs. I want you to get up right now and go to the window, open it and stick your head out and yell, I'm as mad as hell and I'm not going to take this anymore. Things have got to change. You've got to get mad. I want you to get up right now, sit up, go to the window and yell I'm as mad as hell and I'm not going to take this anymore. Then we will figure out what to do about the depression, the inflation and the oil crisis. But first *you've got to get mad.*"

Get *mad?* Yes, indeed. There is a horrendous misconception about getting mad that I would like to clear up right here. We are taught as children and as adults to hold our temper, be nice and don't rock the boat. Acting out in anger is considered rude, embarrassing and threatening. We have become a nation of *Nice.* We have become a complacent society that would rather dissipate inner anger by watching a violent television program, gossiping about a neighbor or stuffing our diseased bodies instead of standing up for what we believe in.

We have a convoluted belief that peace comes to those who never get angry or mad. We vote for candidates based on their calmness and charisma. Heaven forbid if a candidate shows raw, angry emotions and tries to stir people to take action! We want people to be nice. And this is all fine and good, except for the fact that it doesn't change a damn thing. It is not the way to a "Yes!" life.

If we were to measure anger on an energy scale, we would discover on one end, uncontrollable, raging fits of frustration that accelerate into an atomic bomb blast that bursts forth in a disparaging manner and accomplishes nothing but devastation.

In the middle, there's everyday anger that serves to let people know how we feel and is usually expressed in a healthy and nurturing manner.

The light end of the energy scale denotes an anger that is transformative. It is an uppermost powerful energy force, activated by an awareness of Oneness, tempered by acts of forgiveness, courage and surrender and elevated by a relentless, peaceful determination that will absolutely move mountains.

It's Time to Get Mad!

If you want to get something done, get mad. If you want great personal and professional relationships, if you want to improve your golf, bowling or tennis game, if you want prosperity to flow to you, GET MAD. Use the energy of anger to create a "fire in your belly" a sense of determination that says "I can do it! I can do anything!" You may not have thought of anger quite this way before but this is another lesson in valuing and appreciation of the opposite view. Red vs. Blue or Green vs. Yellow, they all support one another.

Consequently your divine anger will support you if you are willing to surrender. Ask yourself, do I want to live a happy, healthy life? Keep asking yourself until you get mad. I want you to stand up right now and go to the window and say, "I'm not going to take it anymore! I am going to do what is right for me! I'm going to live a happy, healthy life!"

I want you to get MAD!

"A day merely survived is no cause for celebration.
You are not here to fritter away your precious hours
when you have the ability to accomplish so much
by making a slight change in your routine."

Og Mandino,
Author of *The Greatest Salesman in the World*

Resource Center

✣ *The Wisdom of Forgiveness: Intimate Conversations and Journeys*, by the Dalai Lama, gives the reader the Buddhist perspective of forgiveness. My favorite excerpt:

"If you have a strong compassion, strong respect for others, the forgiveness is much easier. Mainly for this reason: I do not want to harm another. Forgiveness allows you to be in touch with these positive emotions."

✣ **Websites you may wish to explore:**

www.ofspirit.com

www.cancersupportive care.com

www.explorefaith.org

www.positiveway.com

Ki Exercise # 6

Take a moment to stretch. Stretch your arms above your head then out to your sides. Stretch your torso, back, legs and stretch your toes and fingers by spreading them. Take several deep breaths and let them out.

Close your eyes and relax your body. Use your mind to scan your body for any discomfort or pain. Tighten every muscle you can throughout your entire body. Squeeze it tighter and tighter. Now let it go. Feel the release within your body. Your blood is moving, your skin tingles; the golden light of love in the core of your body is now enlivened. This is the Spirit within everything. This is the Spirit that connects you to the Universe.

Ask your body, "How do you feel?" Listen for answers. Continue to listen as you take another deep breath.

Let yourself relax into the nothingness of Spirit. When a thought comes to mind, examine it. How does it affect your body? How do you feel? How important is it? If thoughts of frustration and worry come to mind, let them go. Let them dissolve into the golden light of love that the Universe supplies. This is your time to let go and surrender to a Higher Spirit. Let yourself trust God and surrender to God's will for you. Breathe in and out and stay as long as you want.

Chapter 7

My Body Is Not Me, but Mine..."Yes!"

"If my body," said Shu, "is not my own, pray whose is it?"
"It is the bodily form entrusted to you by heaven and earth.
Your life is not your own. It is a blend of harmony entrusted
to you by heaven and earth," replied Ch'eng, his tutor.

Chang-tzu

*O*kay, let's get crackin' and get down to the nitty-gritty. It's time to move deeper into the heart of self-leadership and self-healing. What I have shared with you so far has increased your awareness. You're aware of the uniquely different personality styles and how these styles support and actually demonstrate the power of *oneness*. You've learned to access and utilize this information to your advantage. And, most importantly, you have gained awareness of the strength of courage and the power of forgiveness.

Yet it will do you no good whatsoever to be aware of these elements if you can't easily put them to good use. Many people absorb wisdom by reading every self-help book that comes along. They can recite the "wisdoms" of Wayne Dyer, Deepak Chopra, Marianne Williamson and Oprah Winfrey. They can tell you what they've read, but when you talk to them, do you see the results of that knowledge in their eyes? Do they understand it sufficiently to apply it to their own circumstances? It's one thing to *know* and yet another to *do*.

In this chapter, I will share with you what I consider to be the key to taking action and utilizing the wisdom you've gained. What I am about to share with you is something so powerful and yet so simple; and if you are willing to practice just a little, it will change your life forever. In order to become the self-healer and leader of your life, in order to lose weight and gain a healthy body, in order to raise your level of prosperity and create loving relationships, and in order to make a difference in the world, you must be willing to go deeper, deeper into your own bliss, deeper into loving yourself unconditionally.

The best way to accomplish this is to become aware of—and to fully appreciate—the masterpiece you call a body. Although the body, mind and soul are an inseparable system of checks and balances, it's a good idea to spend a moment getting acquainted with your *Body*.

The Body Review

As you move along the path to improved health and overall wellbeing, you'll need guidelines to help you achieve measurable results. The *Body Review* will provide you with an objective analysis that will allow you to recognize your progress. As you go through the questionnaire, listen to what your body is communicating to you. Breathe in deeply, then breathe out as you take a moment to assess your body from *your* perspective. Read each statement and decide how closely it matches your physical and emotional condition. Circle a number, on a scale of 1 through 10, with 10 most likely to match your current situation, and number 1 least likely to match your condition.

LEAST LIKELY TO MATCH (1) ———→ (10) MOST LIKELY TO MATCH

I feel anxious.	1 2 3 4 5 6 7 8 9 10
I have cold hands and cold feet.	1 2 3 4 5 6 7 8 9 10
I have shortness of breath.	1 2 3 4 5 6 7 8 9 10

I find it hard to sleep.	1 2 3 4 5 6 7 8 9 10
I feel fatigued.	1 2 3 4 5 6 7 8 9 10
I get so angry I feel I will explode.	1 2 3 4 5 6 7 8 9 10
I use drugs or alcohol frequently.	1 2 3 4 5 6 7 8 9 10
I sometimes have heart palpitations.	1 2 3 4 5 6 7 8 9 10
I have indigestion.	1 2 3 4 5 6 7 8 9 10
I have migraine headaches.	1 2 3 4 5 6 7 8 9 10
I have lower back pain.	1 2 3 4 5 6 7 8 9 10
I find it hard to slow down and relax.	1 2 3 4 5 6 7 8 9 10
I have tight shoulders muscles.	1 2 3 4 5 6 7 8 9 10
I have allergies.	1 2 3 4 5 6 7 8 9 10
I overeat.	1 2 3 4 5 6 7 8 9 10
I have a loss of appetite.	1 2 3 4 5 6 7 8 9 10

Your total will range from 16-160. This score doesn't determine a *winner* (because we all know you're a winner). This review is meant solely to help you understand where stress lives within your body, so you can begin to take action to alleviate it.

I Have A Question for You...

Let's say you're in the market for a body. (And no, it's not a matter of turning in the old body for a new one.) Instead, I just want you to look at your body as if you were shopping for a boat. After all, your body is the vessel for your soul and in order to fulfill your soul's desire to say "Yes!" to life, you will want to give your body every advantage. Compare these two advertisements and then answer this question: which one of these vessels most closely matches the body you desire?

FOR SALE:

One Wooden Boat: Single hull, soft-construction, one hardwood comfy seat, includes two oars. Recommended for short excursions, this vessel is equipped with one-wet-finger-in-the-wind navigational system. Weathered many storms, but does have a tendency to tip over easily. There's a tune from the Broadway show, *Guys and Dolls*, which comes to mind here: *Sit Down, Sit Down You're Rocking the Boat.* However, if there's one positive thing that could be said about this boat, *it does float!*

Maintenance: We suggest you keep sandpaper, paint, chewing gum, duct tape and several tubes of caulking handy at all times.

Name of the boat: The "NOYADONT"

❈ ❈ ❈

For Sale:

One Durable Yacht: This finely crafted yacht is devoted to the style, precision and luxury of a Rolls-Royce and the performance of a Mercedes. A state of the art GPS navigational system, a wide-beam fiberglass hull and twin 800-horsepower Caterpillar engines provide balance to calm any rough sea of your journey. Attention to the minutest detail; real woodworking, features stainless and marble counters. Ideal for family retreats to hidden Caribbean coves or spirited weekend jaunts with friends.

Maintenance: Although it may cost a pretty penny, this vessel is well worth it.

Name of the boat: The "YESIBE"

So what shivers your timbers, mate? What floats your boat? Are you ready to sign on the dotted line for the "NOYADONT" or the

"YESIBE"? Are you interested in the soft-sided wooden boat with two oars or the magnificent yacht, outfitted with the latest state-of-the-art equipment? Or are you like most of us, somewhere in between? Stop! Before you grab a mirror and give yourself forty lashes and begin counting the extra pounds, sags, bags and wrinkles; I want you to remember one thing.

*My body is not **me**, but **mine**.*

This is not about outward appearances. It is about gaining strength and balance from within, by understanding that *you* are at the helm of your soul's vessel. *You* are in charge of your body. *You* have everything you need for your soul's journey. This ship has been well supplied. Stocked with billions of cells; this magnificent body has the intelligence to heal itself and heal others. You don't have to earn a degree or have a miraculous spiritual epiphany occur before you become captain of your ship. You only have to be willing to take the wheel and say "Yes!" to body, mind and soul.

"The natural forces within us are the true healers of disease."
Hippocrates 400 B.C.

Before I share this powerful and yet simple approach to self empowerment, I want you to know that there is an easy way to gain this knowledge—and a hard way. Let me tell you about the hard way first, so you don't have to go there.

Born to Be Wild

My plan in the summer of '63 was to carhop at the Humdinger, a local teenage hang-out, whereby I would devour free burgers, cherry cokes and licorice shakes. The only other thing to do on hot, sultry nights in Red Bluff, California, was to drag the great five miles of main street, moon your friends and pick-up boys before the streets rolled up at twelve midnight.

At nineteen, sipping beer with my friends in a '59 red Chevy convertible was not only a rite of passage, it was the way this farm girl could act out "born-to-be-wild." Unconscious to the fact that some of our friends never made it to their eighteenth birthday, we all thought we were cool, free and positively destined for greatness.

That summer, a long break between college semesters, lost its coolness when I complained of an earache and was whisked into Dr. Wolfe's office.

"We need to schedule her for surgery immediately." The doctor and my mother exchanged glances.

"Surgery?" To me surgery was getting my big toe lanced after stepping on some old rusty thing in the middle of a wheat field. I had no idea what was in store for me.

Waking from surgery the next day, a wariness come over me, I brushed my hand across my forehead and felt the woven gauze and strips of tape covering my entire face. My anxiety intensified even more when I overheard two nurses talking, "Don't give her a mirror; we don't want to scare her."

When the bandages came off a few days later, I was handed a mirror. A drainage tube flopped along my swollen neck where my shoulder used to be and my right eye didn't close. One half of my head was shaved and numb. My Frankenstein nose, eyebrows and lips had shifted to the left side of my face, making it all so very eerie. Removing a tumor from my salivary gland, the doctors had severed most of the nerves and muscles in my face, leaving me deformed, dumbfounded and downright cartoon scary.

I read the message hidden behind Mom's sigh and smiling tears. "Well, it *is* cancer, but they think they got it all." Sigh. "Everything is going to be all right, honey." My heart sank in disbelief—cancer, "The Big C." Mom had no idea what to say to me and there was no counselor to come to our aid. We coped with it the best we knew how and that meant we just avoided spending too much time on questions we didn't know the answers to. At that time, Cancer (as AIDS is now) was considered to be somewhat contagious and certainly a death sentence.

This is not what I'd planned, it just wasn't fair. Alone in the darkness, panic crept into my thoughts as I planned for my demise. I wrote out my will, leaving my Elvis Presley records, poodle skirts, and forty-five phonograph to my brothers. That took all of five minutes.

Then I began to cry, "Why me, why me? I will never get to finish school or have a normal life."

"Sure you will honey," reassured my mother.

"Yabut, I was going to be Miss Tehama County, now I look like Miss Frankenstein."

"Yabut, I'm not very smart and I'll never finish college." I yammered on.

"Yabut, I'm only nineteen, it's just not fair, why me?" Like a master chef seasoning a pot of gloom, I tended my "sorry soup."

One evening at dinner, my father forcefully put down his fork and said "Yabut! Yabut! Judy, I should call you Nanna Yabut! Snap out of it. Just learn to make the best of the hand you've been dealt. Have you tried exercising your face…getting the muscles to work again?"

My dad, the strong silent type, knew what pushed my buttons. He encouraged me to face my limitations (no pun intended), and to get on with whatever life was ahead of me. Healed faced or no healed face I was going to do *something*.

An overstuffed, shaggy, purple chair and The Ed Sullivan Television Show became therapy headquarters. Smile-stretching laughter exercised my stiff, swollen face and I practiced until my lips began to work. Months later, my eye closed properly to keep the shampoo suds out. The muscles across my forehead and nose had worked their way back to center. And Miss Frankenstein disappeared.

"The latest research indicates," Dr Wolfe affirmed, "that there is no known treatment for this kind of cancer." Then he added something that was cemented in my mind forever, "I suggest you just say 'Yes' to life and go out and live it the best you can." So I did.

It wasn't until seven years later, when I was married and the mother of two babies, a family friend who worked in the doctor's office let the secret slip, "The doctor gave you only two years to live." I've often wondered what would have happened if I'd heard the two-year verdict immediately after surgery.

"There is nothing that the body suffers that the soul may not profit."
George Meredith, 1885

My Dad's love and quick-witted humor taught me two important lessons that all of us need to become the healer and leader of our life. First, it doesn't matter how you *feel* or what you *look* like. Feelings and appearances change as often as the nature of wind. If feelings and appearances determined happiness, my mop-head hair and unbrushed teeth would keep me in bed every morning. *Attitude* is the one thing— the only thing—that directly affects your health, wealth and success; it's the one aspect over which you have immediate control.

The second lesson I learned, once I'd moved away from my dysfunctional family and acquired a dysfunctional family of my own was that life is not perfect. We are all trying to live the best we know how. Some of us suck at it, many of us muddle through, but *no one* has the master key for a successful life. The important things in life are family, friends and the energy of love that heals anything.

That crisis point, when I was just nineteen, was the first time I woke up and took charge of my life, at least for one brief spell. After that, I fell asleep at the wheel again and, as I shared with you in the introduction, I woke up twenty years later, facing cancer once again, as a wife, mother, teacher, and basketball chauffer for two teenagers. The point I want to make here is that *you have the power within you to change or improve anything, if you are willing to be open to new ideas and say "Yes!" to* **your** *life.*

That point is reached when you realize that your body is the vessel for your precious soul, and your precious soul is crying out for you to wake up and do the right thing; to be an instrument of peace, to transform everyday worry, angst and chaos into peace and harmony. Your body is a carrier for your great intentions, and as such, it needs your unconditional love and respect. What it's going to take is your willingness and regular practice in saying, "**'Yes!'** *My body is not* **Me**, *but* **Mine**"

"Body and soul are not two substances but one.
They are man becoming aware of himself two different ways."
C.F. von Weizsacher

Body Is Not Me, But Mine

As it is with personality styles, your body is also a complex system of parts that interact to support the oneness and wholeness of all the other parts. I could go on for a days describing the scientific proof of how your big toe supports your gallbladder, but that's not what I think is important for you to know.

There is an abundance of anatomy, acupuncture and massage books to assist you in learning more about how different parts of your body interrelate. And there is probably a hundred times that in diet and exercise books explaining what foods and movements are good for what body parts.

This is helpful and practical information and I encourage you to read as much as possible about the workings of your body, because knowledge is supreme. But I want to introduce you to something you are better off experiencing rather than reading about—energy.

Ki Energy: The Life Force of The Cosmos

Energy, specifically Ki energy is coursing through your body right now. In fact, it *is* your body. Ki energy moves in and out of your body when you breathe, eat, and dream. Whether you are asleep or awake, Ki is cosmic energy. It is the life force of the cosmos. We can only try to imagine the invisible; however scientific research has proven that it is this invisible energy that makes everything possible. Civilizations seek its essence through many different terms and phrases: *God force, the life force, Brahman, a kind of primordial glue*, or the personal energy know as *Ki* (sometimes written as *Qi* or *Chi*). Many consider it the basis of electro-magnetic energy.

This flow of energy is a continuous progression, one which gives vitality to the body. An overfed, inactive, inflexible body; weak or sick organs are symptoms of an impaired flow of energy. This imbalance can lead to ill health. Many of us barely exist, operating on a minimum of life force. And as we grow older, the life force dwindles until we die. It doesn't have to be that way.

Oh sure we're all going to die, no doubt about it. Nevertheless, it's how you live that really counts. It's how you say "Yes!" to life.

Humanity has become too smart. The day we invented the wheel, we became immersed in technology and, from there, we began the slow and steady process of disassociating ourselves from the Ki forces of life. There is, however, a way to reconnect and expand your connection with cosmic Ki energy.

Understanding The Body's Energy Fields

Eastern philosophers have believed for centuries that your body has thirteen subtle energy fields, called *chakras*. Western medicine has begun to incorporate some of this information into mainstream healing practices, through acupuncture and acupressure. *Chakra* is the Sanskrit word for "wheel" and this word was chosen because the sages described these energy fields as fast moving vortices at the center of physical and psychic energy. Six of the chakras are minor in their activities and seven are major. For our purposes, we will concentrate on the major chakras, plus two significant minor ones.

As the life force enters the body, it passes through and activates these chakras. The human spine is regarded as the mystical link between God and man. The chakras are seen as Ki energy storage centers. The first chakra is located at the base of the spine and represents man's lowest, earthly nature; the uppermost chakra is located at the top of the skull and symbolizes the highest spirituality.

Each chakra relates to the endocrine system and to a specific organ, which is influenced by that chakra's energy field. Chakras can be thought of as dynamos, through which energy is received and transmitted. Each of the chakras vibrates at a characteristic frequency and has been described to be predominately of a certain color which corresponds to the frequency of the vibration.

These energy fields are your key to understanding the concept of "my body is not *me*, but *mine*." Your body is yours to love and to be used to communicate your true self; it is not *all* of you. The name, location and energy benefit of each chakra is described as follows:

The Chakras

Name: First Chakra
Location: Base of the spine
Color: Red

Energy Benefit: The "root" chakra is related to survival and procreation; this energy is connected to the sacral plexus, the rectum, the prostate gland and the male reproductive organs. Considered to be the origin of all sexual energy, this *Kundalini* or physical chakra, once stimulated, ascends the spinal column and activates the remaining chakras.

Name: Second Chakra
Location: Three fingers' width below the navel.
Color: Orange

Energy Benefit: Considered the dwelling place of the self, this chakra or energy center is related to well-being, immunity from disease and the pleasure in life. In Eastern traditions it is thought to govern the impulses of creativity, sexuality and generate physical energy. Life begins in our mother's womb, which we can identify with our personal power.

Name: Third Chakra
Location: Slightly above the navel.
Color: Yellow

Energy Benefit: This power chakra is called the "abdominal brain" because it is a place where we carry our emotions and make decisions. Associated with the solar plexus, spleen, pancreas, liver and gallbladder; this spiritual and physical energy reservoir gives strength to all the other chakras and keeps them healthy.

Name: Fourth Chakra
Location: Center of the chest
Color: Green

Energy Benefit: The heart chakra is connected to the cardiac plexus, the thymus gland and the pericardium. It controls respiration and it also relates to unconditional acceptance, joyfulness and love. There are three chakras above it and three chakras below. It is in this place where the energies of the mind, body and spirit bridge the physical and spiritual plane.

Name: Fifth Chakra
Location: Center of the throat
Color: Blue

Energy Benefit: The throat chakra relates to the thyroid gland and regulates the basal metabolism (the amount of energy used by the body at rest). In Eastern traditions it is said to be associated with creativity and self-expression. It controls speech and sound and therefore is the gateway to authentic communication.

Name: Sixth Chakra
Location: Center of forehead
Color: Indigo

Energy Benefit: The third eye chakra relates to intuition, paranormal powers and psychic awareness. This chakra controls the autonomic nervous system and is associated with the pineal gland which is located between the eyebrows.

Name: Seventh Chakra
Location: Top of Head
Color: Violet

Energy Benefit: The crown chakra relates to the liberation, beyond all elements, into the cosmic energy realm. This chakra corresponds with the pituitary gland and the cortical layer of the brain. When this energy center is opened, supreme bliss and universal energy flow, and all other chakras flow upward to meet the top of the head.

Name: Eighth and Ninth Chakras
Location: Palm of Hands and Center of Feet
Color: White

Energy Benefit: Though considered "minor" chakras, these are extensions to life. By the simple act of reaching out to others, energy is sent and received. When the other chakras are in balance healing energy flows easily and powerfully from you to others and back again.

Now You Need to Have "The Conversation"

Once you are acquainted with the influence and power of chakras, it's time for "The Conversation."

No, this is not the place where the wife says to her spouse, "We need to talk."

"The Conversation" I allude to is the secret to self-empowerment. Unlike any other form of communication, when Ki is recognized, nurtured and allowed to flow freely through the body, the body-mind-spirit connection is strengthened. That means you can do things you never thought possible before.

What Are You Saying to Your Body?

Most other organisms seem naturally to do a better job with this energy than humans do. For instance, plants perform daily magic—creating their own food—from the raw elements in dirt, water and sunlight. Or consider the ant: without benefit of steroids or weight-training or high-tech machinery, this tiny insect manages unceremoniously to carry an object many times bigger and heavier than itself, up a vertical stone surface. How inefficient we are in comparison! How do they do it? Are they tapping into Ki energy in a way we can only dream of?

Every day, every second of the day, you are having a conversation with your body, whether you are aware of it or not. As long as you are alive and inhabit your body you will continue to have a conversation, or in fact, most likely two different conversations simultaneously. So what is it you're saying to your body?

❧ Conversation Number One:

Your outer conversation is all about the ego part of you being good enough. It goes like this:

How do I look? Is there spinach between my teeth? Bad Hair Day! I wish I looked like Julia Roberts. Will Charlie like me if I have a wart on the end of my nose? If only I were smart enough (or rich enough or pretty enough), I'd stop worrying what others think.

Take a little advice from Judge Judy Sheindlin's book title, *Beauty Fades, Dumb is Forever*. Beauty does fade. Years from now it won't matter whether Charlie liked you or you had a bad hair day. And when you allow these thoughts to dominate your thinking you will stay dumb forever.

⚅ Conversation Number Two

This is the conversation you have with your soul: I love myself; I'm great just the way I am. I am so grateful that my body expresses and receives love. I am overflowing with energy as I listen to the subtle vibrations of body energy. I touch my soul as my body is nurtured and loved.

The primary purpose we are on this planet, in this form, is to learn to grow our soul. Our soul yearns for us to open to our true selves and experience the peace and grace that comes from being of service. We are here to make this world a better place by our presence. What is the main vessel to help you accomplish this? Voilà, your body!

"You are the master of your life. Body is not you but yours. All you need is practice. Life is a practice, so what are you practicing?"
Master UGene

Having The Conversation Daily

Eventually your goal will be to communicate intimately with your body and be able to direct health-giving energy to a specific area. Just as a laser emits a highly focused beam of energy that utilizes certain substances to absorb electromagnetic energy, you too, with practice, will be able to direct your energy precisely. This may sound far-fetched but, trust me, you can do this. You have within you the power, capability and potential to use your Ki energy to rectify, settle and naturally restore any imbalance.

However, like any skill, it takes training and practice. Life is training. Your brain needs the repetition of practice to build confidence in your abilities. So here are a few fun and easy exercises to practice, so you can become more aware of your body's Ki energy and how it interacts with your environment.

SAY "YES!" TO LIFE

Feng Shui Your Environment

Feng Shui, the alignment and balance of your home environment, will also help you to find alignment and balance within your body. Your state of mind, good or ill, affects your environment. This exercise is an excellent method for simultaneously becoming aware of the inner and outer spaces around you. Practice this and it will become second nature for you to see the balance in all things around you.

Sit or stand in the center of the room. Let your posture be balanced and relaxed. Breathe naturally and calmly. Concentrate on the center of your body, and gently let go of your thoughts. Just be in the space, without preconceptions about it. Next simply walk about the space for awhile. Let your intuition respond and give you impressions. Where is there more energy? Where is there less energy? Where is the energy more powerful? Where is it positive? Where is it negative? Try this in different rooms of your home. It may take awhile but you will get the knack of it.

Soul Food: Eat Foods That Rot

In order to have a healthy mind and easy access to your Spirit and Ki energy you must feed the body energizing food in an energizing way. With the hustle and bustle of everyday contemporary life, it is difficult to find time to eat in peace. We eat in our cars, at our desks, in front of the TV. Although I still make an effort to work this into my schedule, my suggestions are as follows:

Pour a favorite cup of tea; warm tea will help your digestive system. Choose fresh, energized food and prepare it ahead to give you more time to enjoy it at your leisure. Sit quietly and take a moment to appreciate the food in front of you. Now take a deep cleansing breath, then let it out and relax. Slowly take one bite—and put your fork down. Close your eyes and focus on the flavors and textures. Food should please all five senses. Take a sip of tea. Notice how it feels in your mouth then swallow. Take another bite and repeat. Sit quietly for a few minutes after eating.

"To keep the body in good health is a duty…otherwise we shall not be able to keep our mind strong and clear."

Buddha

Brush Your Hair And Comb Your Teeth

Body hygiene and grooming is a perfect time to get in touch with your body's Ki energy. The next time you are brushing and combing, take a moment to observe the magnificent creature called You.

For some of you this may feel uncomfortable. That's a good sign; if you are uncomfortable you're growing.

Closely examine your face in the mirror. What do you see? Look deeply into your eyes, for they are the window to your soul. Spend time admiring your skin, eyes, nose, ears and hair. Before you go to work or before bed try this exercise to enliven your brain and body as you gaze at your magnificence.

Tapping to Beauty

Using both hands let your fingers dangle loosely as you begin briskly tapping the top of your head, thirty times. Tap around to your forehead, thirty times. Now down to your jaw line, twenty times. Now to the back of your head; this will stimulate your occipital area. Tap down at the base of your skull, neck, and then shoulders. Feel the subtle vibration and awakening of your body. You are ready for your day.

"The body has a mind of its own."

Mason Cooley

Do You Own The Computer?

It is said that if you sit at a computer long enough, it owns you. Since the human spine is regarded as the mystical link between God and man, and the chakras are the storage centers for Ki, it's understandable that by sitting on your tush, crunching up your spine all day in front of a computer will block your energy fields. Here are some simple exercises to do at your desk to revitalize your energy and open your spine.

Compute to Stretch

Stand up. Take a deep breath and let it out. Clasp your hands together and stretch your arms above your head. Continue to stretch, as you attempt to open your chest chakra and let your shoulder blades touch. Slowly and easily bend backward as far as you can. Bring your arms down to your sides. Take another deep breath and let it go. Bend your body at the waist and let your arms drop and swing like a monkey. (You can make primate sounds if you like.) As you focus on the seven chakras stretch your spine and try to touch your toes. Do this several time to revitalize your entire body.

Meditation, The Internal Tool

Meditation allows us to quiet the mind in order to see one's self more clearly. The big question is, how, exactly do you keep the mind quiet? Most people who give up trying to meditate do so because they aren't able to stop their mind chatter. However there are many approaches to calming the mind and one or more of these may work well for you: listening to one hand clap, holding gemstones, reading affirmation cards, praying with a rosary. Whatever gives you a quiet mind is what is best for you.

> *"Meditation is the brain's way of 'breathing deeply.'"*
> Ilchi Lee

Have you ever sat around a campfire with good friends, sharing good conversation? You may have noticed that occasionally all conversation ceases and a comfortable silence takes hold. As you gaze into the flames, your mind wanders, as it is both tied down and released at the same time by the fascination of the dancing, glowing vision before you. At such a point, your logical mind might relax into a creative state, which may produce new insights and conversations. But during some of the silence, you may have slipped into a true meditative state, where you simply are not holding a conscious thought in your mind. It is an easy, fun way to relieve stress and get your body and mind to a calm, empty state.

Hoedown Slap Down

Start at your shoulders and firmly—without hurting yourself—begin slapping your left shoulder with your right hand thirty times. Moving down your arm, continue slapping until you get to the top of your hand. Clap your two hands together ten times. Now turn your left arm over, palm up, and begin slapping your way back up to your shoulder. Do the same on the other side of your body, working your way back up to your right shoulder. Follow your meridian channels or chakra energy points in your body down to second chakra or energy center (three fingers' width below the navel). Bring your mind to this area and continue tapping thirty or more times. Your mind and body are energized. Now find your favorite meditation corner and listen to your body's subtle vibrations. Your mind is empty now and your body is calm.

Practice Your Intangible Joy

He had performed at the Bath Opera House, an amateur opera company staging a small number of productions each year. He managed to scrape together enough money to attend some master classes in Italy. But as one expert put it, "A few master classes, even with the great man, do not constitute 'a formal opera training' by any stretch of the imagination."

As a mobile phone salesman, he had never earned a penny from an opera performance and yet there Paul Potts stood on the stage of Britain's Got Talent television program, proclaiming to thousands, "I've come to sing opera, I want to make a living at what I love."

Reservations crossed the judges' minds as the orchestra swelled and this disheveled, geeky-looking dreamer began to peal the opening notes of Puccini's famous aria, Nessun Dorma. But before he'd finished, the entire audience was on its feet, moved to tears by a truly tender and glorious experience. Paul Potts, the unlikely looking opera wannabe, went on to win the competition, and our hearts.

He was not a professional opera singer pretending to be a mobile phone salesman, but rather a mobile phone salesman aspiring to be a professional opera singer through the diligence of practice.

This is what comes forth when a person is in contact with all of his or her Ki energy. We see a breathtaking vision of love, passion, risk, emotions and the intangible thing that causes joy.

By focusing on your body's subtle energies or chakras, you experience the joy of being fully present in the moment. Don't wait for a special occasion; this you can do while washing dishes, paying bills, watching TV, preparing a meal, walking the dog or mowing the lawn.

When you are focused on your body you are in the present moment. The present moment is not yesterday nor is it tomorrow. It is occurring right now. Therefore there is nothing—neither the past nor the future—standing in the way of you saying "Yes!" to life. You are living the moment and unconditionally loving the moment.

Resource Center

Human Technology: A Toolkit for Authentic Living, by Ilchi Lee, shares information about how life really works, and the importance of understanding "the body is not me, but mine." My favorite quote:

"Most of us have become detached from what being truly healthy means; individually, or as the collective that we call 'society,' until our health is taken away from us in a dramatic moment of diagnosis by a specialist, or our collective health is threatened by the actions of terrorists, corporations or governments."

Ki Energy for Everybody, by Louise Taylor and Betty Bryant, provides solid information about the way Ki energy works in the body, as well as in everyday life.

Ki Exercise # 7

This special Ki chakras exercise will help you practice daily. Before you start, use the Hoedown Slap Down to relax your body and allow you to focus more easily.

Settle your mind by taking several deep cleansing breaths. If you like, turn on some soothing music to balance the atmosphere. Take a moment to brew your favorite cup of tea. Sip your tea then find a comfortable place to stretch out your body. Some people prefer sitting with their legs crossed while others may prefer to lie down. The important point is to keep the spine straight and relaxed.

Close your eyes.

Breathe in and breathe out. Start at the top of your head, letting your face, jaw, neck, and shoulders loosen up. Let this sensation move through your entire body, clear down to the tip of your toes.

Breathe in and out, then release. Focus your mind on your body's first chakra, at the base of your spine. From this area, imagine a pulsating vibrant red energy rising and filling your body with energy from the earth.

Breathe in and out, then release. Slowly move your attention to your body's second chakra, just below your navel. Imagine a warm, comforting orange glow swirling from this area where you hold the love of life. This important chakra deserves your loving attention; it is your connection to a strong healthy self.

Breathe in and out, then release. Bring your mind to your body's third chakra, slightly above your navel. This area is a reservoir of spiritual and physical energy. It is your "abdominal brain" or intuition. Let the luminous yellow color glow and move throughout your body, going to every organ, and every cell. Breathe in and out, then release.

Slowly bring your attention to the middle of your chest, to the fourth chakra, the heart chakra. Open your heart as you relax and accept unconditional love for your entire body. Let the glowing love of green nurturing light combine with the other colors as you let go of your ego and allow cosmic wisdom bridge the physical and spiritual you.

Breathe in and out, then release. Direct your attention to your body's fifth chakra, the throat chakra. Slowly imagine the color blue radiating soothing and calming energy; creating a peaceful harmonious expression of you. Let your throat relax. Let your life be easy. Let yourself express life.

Breathe in and out, then release. Focus your loving thoughts on your sixth chakra. The colors from all the other chakras have now blended to a pulsating indigo glow. Slowly bring your attention to the center of your forehead. Stay focused on the brilliant indigo color, allowing your mind to increase intuition and psychic awareness.

Breathe in and out, then release. Feel your body. Notice how it is different than when you began this exercise. Straighten your spine and tuck your chin slightly. Sense your aliveness as you now bring your attention to the seventh chakra at the top your head. This crown chakra relates to liberation and is the meeting place of cosmic energy. As you practice awareness of this chakra you will experience more bliss and energy gradually increasing. Breathe in and out, release.

Chapter 8

My Mind Is Not Me, but Mine..."Yes!"

*"The secret of health for body, mind, and soul
is not to mourn for the past, nor to worry about the future,
but to live in the present moment wisely and earnestly."*
Buddha

The other day, at a picnic with friends, the conversation rambled. It started with some dude's awesome t-shirt, moved quickly to food and then to the topic of healthcare. One woman spoke of her lupus as "it's my cross to bear at my age." A younger man shared the many seemingly, unnecessary procedures his mother endured before succumbing to cancer at the age of eighty-five. Talk turned to the high cost of medical care for the insured and the uninsured. Then it swung in a staccato beat to the news of an electromagnetic machine, developed in Europe that instantly zaps cancer from the body and returns it to a natural state of health.

"Well I think," I piped in, "that we treat hospitals and doctors as if we were going to our local garage mechanic. When something breaks down, wears out, needs grease etc., we hand our bodies over to an authority as if he or she knows more than we do about taking care of ourselves. We wouldn't need a large, laborious and impecunious healthcare system to determine our state of health if we relied more on our own inner healing power instead of outside circumstances."

While on my soap box I went on to share a little about the focus of the book I was writing and my own experiences. As it is with most authors that try to sum up, in two minutes, what they've been writing about for months, well... jaws were agape and they looked at me as if I had three heads and one of them was speaking Martian on the third moon of Jupiter.

They understood what I was saying but still believed that the present health care system, although extremely flawed, was the answer to all their healthcare questions. After chewing the fat of that juicy ball of wax for awhile, the energy shifted once more to chastising the pharmaceutical industry, the presidential debates, national politics then spiraled downward until it ran amok and it was time to eat.

The Dis-ease Is Not Mine

This slice of dialogue illustrates the different perspectives people have about staying healthy or regaining their health. Some people identify themselves as their dis-ease such as: *my* lupus, *my* heart attack, *my* blood pressure, *my* cancer etc. That's why I never wanted to go to an inaptly named Cancer Support Group. I didn't want to support my cancer I wanted to heal from it. The dis-ease is not mine; it is something that occurred because of an error in my perception.

John's bit of wisdom summed up our conversation with the truth, "It is up to us to take care of ourselves. We need to decide from our gut what's right. We need to start asking compelling questions to get the result we want. After all, when it's all said and done... if some procedure doesn't work, who will feel the results? YOU!"

I would add that you need is to start asking compelling questions of yourself, your inner self as well as of the medical profession. The medical profession has its place in helping people heal but it is up to us to heal. What you'll require is the ability to make a deep enough connection from the mind to the body and the body to the mind so that your soul has a chance to be heard. Once you are in full communication with your soul; you will know what is good for you and how to proceed.

In this chapter you'll learn how *My Mind Is Not Me, But Mine.* You'll learn practical techniques to help center you mind so as to gain control over the deafening, noisy chatter that keeps you from experiencing your true self and implementing your soul's desires.

Your Mind Is The Mast with A Mainsail

As *your body* is the vessel for your soul, *your mind* is the mast with a mainsail. This is what steers your soul's vessel into the best possible wind, guides you through the storms of life and helps you get the most out of your journey. Your mind's beliefs steer your vessel. Beliefs are powerful and fuel everything! They fuel your thoughts, feelings, what you struggle with and what comes easy. It doesn't matter if you want to heal your body, gain a promotion or attract a healthy relationship, your beliefs are at this moment forming your world.

However, your mind is not you but yours; yours as a precious tool used properly will yield the highest potential for growing and developing your soul's desires. You are not your body neither are you your mind. These are only tools for your use while here on this planet. Imagine all the people in the world running around with their own little tool belt. Everyone is equipped with the same tools; its how they use the tool they are given that counts.

> *"We are free up to a point of choice,*
> *and then the choice controls the chooser."*
>
> Mary Crowly

Everyone knows that negative thoughts affect your body adversely and positive thoughts encourage health. You don't need to correct your thinking by digging into some psychiatrist's couch to find deep-seated coins of wisdom that will right your psyche. (That is, unless you need a major overhaul.) You know by now that you are the only one who has the tools to fix whatever body ailment or unhealthy situation your beliefs may have caused. You are the only one who can change attitudes and therefore change your life circumstance.

Later in this chapter, I'll be sharing seven techniques to empower and help you manage your mind—and therefore your body—to bring both into a peaceful, calm state. To get the most out of these seven techniques it's an excellent idea to first have a baseline of your mind's beliefs.

Let's take a moment to establish a **Mind Is Not Me, But Mine Baseline** so that you can determine what areas of your belief system are fine and what areas may need some adjustment.

My Mind Is Not Me, But Mine Baseline

Breathe in and let go of all the air in your lungs. Relax. Breathe in and breathe out. Clear your mind from all other cares. Ask yourself to what degree (one being low and ten being high) do I believe each of the following statements is true? Make a note about your feeling and thoughts as to why you believe this statement.

LOWEST DEGREE (1) ⟶ (10) HIGHEST DEGREE

1. It is possible to focus my mind to heal my body.
   1   2   3   4   5   6   7   8   9   10

_____

_____

_____

2. It's never too late to start taking care of my mind, body and soul.
   1   2   3   4   5   6   7   8   9   10

_____

_____

_____

3. I can increase my energy level by focusing more on my body.

   1 2 3 4 5 6 7 8 9 10

_____

_____

_____

4. I can change old behaviors or habits if I really want to.
   1 2 3 4 5 6 7 8 9 10

_____

_____

_____

5. When it comes to my mind, I am the master.
   1 2 3 4 5 6 7 8 9 10

_____

_____

_____

6. I know the true purpose for my life.
   1 2 3 4 5 6 7 8 9 10

_____

_____

_____

7. I have a balanced mind and a balanced body to say "Yes!"
   1 2 3 4 5 6 7 8 9 10

_____

_____

_____

8. I can do great things when my mind and body feel connected.
   1 2 3 4 5 6 7 8 9 10

_____

_____

_____

9. I can choose my life purpose; it is not predestined.
   1 2 3 4 5 6 7 8 9 10

_____

_____

_____

10. I am compassionate and understanding with myself and others.
    1 2 3 4 5 6 7 8 9 10

_____

_____

_____

You're A Winner Whatever Your Score Is

Keep in mind your assessments and notes as your read the following suggestions and ideas to increase your ability to utilize, manage and value your emotions.

Keep in mind that *the information I am about to share with you is absolutely useless* if you are not willing to practice saying "YES!" It's up to you. Each of these exercises correlates with your body's energy chakras to help you focus your mind and center your body.

A Grounded Mind

1. Concentrate on Your Strengths

People are most successful when they are matched with activities that they love to do, according to Stanford University study of 250,000 people. The study concluded that high intelligence didn't guarantee high accomplishment. So there is still hope for you and me. Hard work and enthusiasm in the field of choice was the leading indicator of success. Implications for you: instead of spending time trying to correct weaknesses, focus on developing your strengths from the inside out. Here's a way to do it:

Pick one thing to strengthen. Excellence is the product of practicing what you like doing. Focus in on one thing that you like doing and then practice doing it the best you can each day. You may find it difficult or challenging but stick with it. Align your attention with your intention and you will grow stronger and more confident from within.

Ignore weaknesses and recognize your self importance. Deal with only those problems that lessen your productivity. Your strengths will overpower your weaknesses when you recognize and appreciate your worthiness. Remember self-esteem comes before peer-esteem because you count first.

First Chakra: Take a deep breath from deep inside your body. Focus on your tailbone area as you let go and take another breath. Visualize your connection to the center of the earth. This is where your strength originates. Stay in the present moment as you imagine gathering strength from the core of the earth up through your spine. Let the warm red glow permeate your entire body as you relax and focus on the energy of the color red. Clear your mind of all other thoughts as you go deeper and deeper into your strengths.

2. Constant Craving Mind

There is a constant craving inside everyone; we are all yearning and searching to better ourselves. To satisfy these cravings you must take risks. This valuable information will assist in understanding what kind of risk taker you are and how you can expand your tolerance for risk without falling apart like some half-baked-dough boy. The two best ways to change your tolerance level for risk is to listen carefully to your choice of words:

Low risk tolerance language clues:

- I don't like to make waves.

- What will I do if things go wrong?

- I don't like to work without a specific result.

High risk tolerance language clues:

- I like the freedom to do a job the way I think it should be done.

- Nothing is ever for certain anyway.

- I accept change as a welcome friend.

Expand Your Risk Threshold By Taking Small Steps

The first step is to listen to your words and emotions and correct your perceptions about risk whenever possible. Your risk meter weighs your risks according to your beliefs. Are you trying to please others or are you listening to your intuition? Here's one of my favorite quotes:

"But risks must be taken, because the greatest hazard in life
is to risk nothing. The person who risks nothing, does nothing,
has nothing and is nothing. They may avoid suffering and sorrow
but they cannot learn, feel change, grow, love or live.
Chained by their attitudes they are slaves; they have
forfeited their freedom. Only the person who risks is free."
Anonymous Chicago Teacher

💧 **Second Chakra:** Breathe in and release all air possible. Focus on the radiance of the orange energy. Imagine it pulsating throughout your body. This is where your creative impulses are sparked, your sexual energy is quickened and your ability to take qualified risks. Focus your mind on your energy center (two inches below your bellybutton.) Let go of fear and doubt, relax, and center your mind-body and Spirit to allow yourself to say "Yes!" to the pleasures you desire and deserve.

3. Liquid Mind

For years I've asked my family to try a number of wacky things. I'm always experimenting on someone or something—part of being a risk taker I guess. So now I'm asking you to try something.

In his book, *The Hidden Messages of Water*, Dr. Masaru Emoto uses high-speed photography to show how frozen water crystals change when exposed to specific messages such as "thank you so much" or "you damn fool." He demonstrates water's unique role in transporting the natural vibration of words and thoughts.

An Experiment: Water's Role in Transmitting Thought Energy

Our bodies consist of 90% water. We depend on water for our very existence and the energy of water is as invisible as the subtle energies of our body—something to think about. Try this experiment to see the affect your thoughts have on water.

Purchase two large yellow or white onions. Find two same size drinking glasses. On one, write a positive message; on the other, a negative. Pour equal amounts of water into each glass. Place an onion (root base down but not touching the water) on top of each glass. Place them away from direct sunlight and check them periodically, comparing the two. From my experience, the onion in the glass with the positive messages will grow faster. But try it for yourself and see what happens.

✷ **Third Chakra:** Breathe in, let your mind go. Focus on the brilliance of yellow as you let go of negative thoughts to grow healthy. This area relates to your emotions and decision making. This is where you decide the type of energy or words you want to influence your body, mind and Spirit. Breathe in, breathe out and let yourself bathe in and appreciate your precious mind, your precious body and your precious Spirit.

4. Generous Mind

Whenever we do good deeds for others with no strings attached our sense of intrinsic worth and self-esteem increase. It has also been known to change the energy of an entire company. Giving helps us gain insight, understanding and promotes the power of love. One of the most powerful things you can do is become selfless in your service to others. Here are a few ideas that can help get you started:

- Drop off cookies at a senior citizens' home.

- When you finish mowing your lawn, mow your neighbor's.

- Pay for the groceries of the person behind you in line.

- Clean your child's bedroom and then claim the gnome that lives in the attic did it.

- Place ten one-dollar bills in ten envelopes and mail them to people from the phone book.

- Crochet or knit scarves, hats, sweaters etc. for the homeless.

- Send affirmation cards to strangers or unsigned birthday cards to people you know.

✷ **Fourth Chakra:** Focus once again on the energy chakras of your body; breathe in and out. Here is where the energies of the mind, body and Spirit come together to form a perfect union. Bring the energy of your first, second and third chakras to mind as you appreciate the magnificence of how they support each other. In the center of your chest is your heart chakra; vivaciously open to love and compassion for yourself and others. Feel the energy come over you as you focus on the magnificent green energy that spreads throughout your body and down your arms to your giving and receiving hands.

5. Affirming Mind

Affirmations are powerful tools. The energetic vibration of thought is the reason affirmative words work. Many people tell me they've tried affirmations, insisting they don't work for them. As with all things in life, it's how you practice that counts. Here are a few suggested ways to use affirmations to assist you in changing your mind and thereby a habit or behavior.

Test An Affirmation

Write out your chosen affirmation on a piece of paper. For instance: *Live the law of love* or *I am worth it* or *I forgive myself.* Change the words until you feel strongly about what you are affirming. Say them out loud or to yourself fifty times. Take them into your mind and "soak" with them.

Places for Affirmations

Bathroom mirrors, refrigerator, desk top, car console, dinner table, ceiling, treadmill, bicycle, back of chairs, coffee table, bottled water or anywhere you can see them frequently.

🔯 **Fifth Chakra:** Take a deep breath and sit with the affirming words you have chosen. Let the blue energy of centered communication and self expression surround you as you allow the words to sink into your consciousness. Now interlock your thumbs and forefingers to form a chain. Bring the word or phrase to mind and attempt to pull your fingers apart. If they stay locked together theses are words that you believe will help you. Just to prove this works test yourself by stating a negative thought and try to pull your fingers apart. Your body is communicating with your mind and your Spirit is waking up to say "Yes!" Continue to test all your thoughts as you focus on your throat area and breathe.

6. Loving Mind

David R. Hawkins M.D., Ph.D., author of Power vs. Force: The Hidden Determinants of Human Behavior writes, "Conversely, the person who has arrived at a habitual state of *unconditional Love* will find anything less to be unacceptable. As one advances in the evolution of his individual consciousness, the process starts to perpetuate and correct itself so that self-improvement becomes a way of life."

A loving mind, a habitual state of unconditional love, evolves from your willingness to trust your intuition and thereby consciously view life though a loving mind.

Enlarge Your Capacity to Love Unconditionally

The attitude and energy of unconditional Love is attainable right here, right now. Here are five suggestions to enlarge your capacity to love unconditionally.

- Express true compassion for yourself and others.

- Use your intuition to sense the energy of a room or person.

- Accept peace as an attainable goal.

- Endeavor to see yourself as a person who loves intuitively from your heart and soul.

- Exercise acceptance; see no differences, only universal love for all, no matter what.

Sixth Chakra: Breath in, breathe out. Visualize the indigo color in the center of your forehead. Peace is all around you. Let go of fear, doubt or worry. Let yourself fall into the neutral zone where everything is nothing and nothingness is everything. In this space of nothingness there is nothing to judge or feel, only peace. Your intuition is enlivened when you are in the neutral zone. From this place you can love all people, places and things unconditionally.

7. Soul-Based Mind

As you practice oneness and gain an understanding of yourself and others, you will develop an ability to live a soul-based life. In other words, you will ask your soul how to live, breathe and be; you will let your soul guide you. You will no longer experience life as an individual person separated from others; you will feel a connectedness to everything. You will live in a neutral space with a clear uncluttered mind. That is the ultimate intended result. In the concept of *My Mind Is Not Me, But Mine*; the mind is merely a tool of consciousness through which your primary value is that of communication. A soul-based mind lets you live from your soul's desires consciously and deliberately.

Suggestions for Utilizing Your Soul-based Mind

- Practice chakra mediation to encourage oneness and wholeness.

- Seek out the good qualities in everyone you meet, no matter what.

- Allow yourself to reach beyond contentment to a blissful, joyful and ecstatic life.

- Realize that there is a cosmic flow of liberating bliss that you can jump into now.

- This bliss will allow you to easily attract the things in life that you need and desire.

Seventh Chakra: Close your mouth and breathe in slowly through your nostrils; let it go. Close your eyes. Focus your mind on the rich, vibrant violet color. Breathe into your neutral zone and let go of all cares. At the top of your head is the universal energy of unconditional love; it needs your permission to come in and feed your soul with supreme bliss. Envision a golden liquid light gently pouring down over your entire body as you open your mind to the unconditional love of the Universe. Let if fill you, complete you and let your mind accept more and more love until you are overcome with bliss. Descend into the comfort of oneness and stay as long as you like.

Keep in Mind

You are developing your awareness of the chakras as you practice each meditation. The chakras-energy centers higher in your body deal more with the spiritual aspects of life whereas the lower chakras nourish the body elements. Try to remember that while you are nurturing your spiritual growth, your head may be in the clouds. However, your body needs you to keep your feet on the ground.

Life is full of experiences that will lead you to discover that My Mind is Not Me but Mine. It can happen in a crowd or when you are alone with your thoughts. You never know where, what or who will inspire you to change your perception of yourself and others.

Swimming with Bambi

The junk-food-stuffing, remote-control-popping insanity of my life was about to end. I was suffering from RCSS (recliner, channel-surfing syndrome). Millions of people suffer and die from this syndrome each year. However, there are studies that have proven that a person can burn the same amount of calories *thinking* about jogging as it takes to jog. I tried that once.

But now, circling the siphon bowl of the abyss, spiraling ever downward into the black hole of re-runs, I had this thought: maybe I should exercise.

To get motivated, I called my friend Melissa and talked her into a water aerobics class. Neither one of us worries about getting too much exercise; our buddy system thinking has a fatal flaw. Guaranteed before too much time passes we'll both come up with more excuses than President Bill Clinton, as to why we can't exercise. Nonetheless we are eternal optimists.

Wrangling a swim suit from moth balls, I stuffed a gym bag, and grabbed the car keys. I was doing all right until I caught a glimpse of myself in the hall mirror. Miss America can rest easy and, for that matter, so can Barbara Walters. Melissa says she has it on good authority that there's a diva body snatcher who exchanges body parts from one woman to another. This is true because I know for a fact that these are not the thighs I started out with. I'm sure some babe has my left hip and flat stomach. In my mind, I'm twenty-five, slim, trim and fit. And indeed, it is what I think of myself that really matters.

Through the chlorine, sweet perfumes, and anti-perspirant mist that encircled the pool's dressing room I gasped in horror, "Melissa! Melissa! Melissa! My suit shrunk! It fit last year!"

With what can only be described as a devious smile she replied, "Give it a little yank, maybe you can stretch it."

I wanted to turn around and go home. How did I allow myself to get so out of shape? What must everybody be thinking? With that I drew in a breath and I began having my way with spandex. Climbing the Mount Everest of flab I rolled, tucked, and tugged ripples of cellulite. Exhausted, I rested at the hips. Then exhaling all possible air, I hoisted what little fabric that was left up and over my chest. Yanking the bottom rim down over my butt cheeks caused my boobs to pop out like two white Casabas. But bound and determined, I smooshed, scrunched and squirmed until I reached a point that if I bent my knees and walked like a crippled ostrich, I could make it to the pool.

Buoyancy is a blessing; once in the water I lost thirty five pounds. A sea of white-cotton-puffs (senior citizens) floating and chatting across the aqua ripples set the scene. At the edge of the pool was "Bambi." Twenty if a day, blonde, every muscle and curve in place. Melissa grabbed my arm pulling me back into the water before I could ask Bambi if she had my left hip.

"Okay, class, let's GO!" Bambi twirled, raised her right arm and touched her left toe. The twins, cheerfully overstuffed hippopotami were trying to find their feet. She lost me at "Raise your right arm." We couldn't keep up with the white-cotton-puffs, thirty years our senior.

"Is it time yet?" Melissa pleaded.

"No," I wheezed.

Finally the clock gave up its hour to wobbling rubber knees that toddled behind the white cotton puffs to the showers. All I could think was how out of shape my body was, how ridiculous I looked and where did these lovely senior citizens get all their energy? This was the day I learned something about what self image and self-esteem really means.

White-haired goddesses worshiped the shower head as I waited my turn. They were remarkable. Their bodies bounced but didn't bounce back, their cottage cheese thighs and their wrinkles jiggled. When they stood in front of a mirror they could see their rear end without turning around. And they didn't seem to care. It came to mind that what really mattered was my *perception* and *attitude* toward my body and toward life. All bodies get old and fade but the true beauty lies within. Letting go of feelings of inadequacy and self-consciousness is saying "Yes!" to your true self.

At that moment the Mighty Peewee Swimmers burst through the door like a thunderbolt from Zeus. Talk about an energy shift, whew. The white cotton puffs side-shuffled as the bubbling, squealing and screeching three-year-olds cut the air of austere sublime. High pitched cries enveloped mothers of disrobing tiny tots.

"Hi Jimmy, how are you today?" Gladys greeted.

Jimmy and his brother Tommy had never met a naked stranger. Brimming with eager exuberance and oblivious to their surroundings they were fully alive in the moment. After removing his coat, his mom shooed him toward the stalls, "It's time to go potty, Jimmy."

"I don't wanna," scrunching his face.

"Go potty... go.!" Mom gave him *the look,* "Go now, Jimmy," Kneading his toe into the floor he turned toward the restroom stalls while his mom tended his brother. All too soon he was at her side. She turned to the little faker. "Did you go potty?"

"I don't wanna," he smiled coyly.

"Go, Jimmy. Potty...now!" Mom puffed and pointed. With his head lowered and his feet slapping across the wet floor, he succumbed. Soon Jimmy was at her side once again. Double-checking her ward she asked, "Jimmy did you go potty?"

"Yes!" He beamed.

"Are you sure? Are you really sure?"

Jimmy shrugged, uncrossed his arms and held open his swimming trunks. In a clear and blaring voice, he directed his dialogue to his penis, "We went potty didn't we?"

The room choked on tears of laughter.

My Mind Is Not Me, But Mine

What you believe, what you perceive as your body image, is a reflection of how you perceive the rest of your life experiences. It is up to you to think. What if you had the mind set of a Goddess that has foregone ego to enjoy the water? What if you had the mind set of a child who believes that all his body parts are his friends? What if you sent loving thoughts to your friend, your body? This act alone would change the world.

Your mind is yours; you have the ability to change your perception now. Give it up; you're really enough just the way you are right now. Don't wait until you are some kind of perfect. It's time you put your mind to good use.

Resource Center

The Survivor Personality, by Al Siebert, Ph.D., shares stories and first-class information on the workings of a survivor personality and how you can acquire more of this trait. My favorite quote:

"If you believe it would be useful to change your attitude about negative attitudes, you can. Changing your attitude will not be easy, however. Attitudes are habits. Like all habits, they develop slowly and change slowly."

Anatomy of an Illness, by Norman Cousins

The Science of Being Well, by Wallace D. Wattles— a radical book. It was published in 1910 and it is still as radical today. My favorite quote:

"There is a Cosmic Life which permeates, penetrates and fills the interspaces of the universe, being in and through all things. This life is not merely a vibration or form of energy—it is a Living Substance. All things are made of it. It is All, and in all."

Media Resources & Websites you may want to explore:

- www.mindtools.com
- www.sciam.com
- www.mind.org
- www.scienceofmind.org
- The movie: *A Beautiful Mind* 2001

Ki Exercise # 8

It is time to take time for the most important person on the planet, you. Do the *Hoedown Slap Down,* slapping your body all over, to relax your body and allow your mind to focus more easily.

Gather your favorite cup of tea, sip it slowly, breathe in, breathe out and begin to relax. Sit in a comfortable position, either on the floor or in a chair. Straighten your spine and curl up your tail bone. Close your eyes and let your meandering mind rest; let all your concerns melt away.

Bring your mind to the very base of your spine the tiny tip of your last vertebrae. Visualize a warm red ball of color encircling this area. Feel your strength increase as you focus.

Now bring your mind to the next chakra. Your sexually energy, creativity and impulses are surrounded in orange glowing light in your lower abdomen. Let your mind nurture you and provide you with energetic enthusiastic drive it takes to stay the course and get things done.

Visualize the brilliant yellow color as you focus on your stomach area. Let the energy of this color permeate your body to enliven your intuition and help you make sound decisions.

Bring your focus to the center of your chest and imagine the rich effervescent color of green pulsating and spreading throughout your body. Let it open your heart to the compassion and unconditional love in the world.

Lovingly move your focus to your throat area and imagine a soothing blue ball of light calming your glands and relaxing your communication channel so your heart can express your soul's desires.

Bring your mind to the center of your forehead. Imagine the beautiful indigo color clearing your mind and opening your spiritual awareness. Empty your mind. Let yourself find the space of neutral nothingness. Be open to change

Your soul is waiting for you to say "Yes!" to life. Visualize the soft warm violet color covering the top of your head. Imagine it pouring down over you touching and charging each chakra with universal energy to sustain you in your pursuit of your soul's desires. Now you can begin to open up the soul based life of unconditional love.

You are now prepared to go out into the world: centered, confident, generous and accepting of the lavish, opulent gifts coming your way and you are grateful.

Chapter 9

My Soul Is Me and Mine..."Yes!"

*"Out of the night that covers me, Black as the Pit from pole to pole,
I thank whatever gods may be, For my Unconquerable Soul."*
W.C. Henley, *Invictus*

Y our body is the vessel for your soul, allowing you emotional, physical and spiritual experiences of the world around you. Your mind is the mainsail of your soul, a magnificent free-wheeling instrument catches the winds of love, drama, fear and peace at your whim. Your soul, however, is not interested in what you think or how you feel. Just as a compass points to true north, so your soul points to your true self. Its only interest is unfolding and expressing its authentic nature.

Why Is It So Important to Listen to Your Soul?

Why bother digging any deeper, searching your soul by paying attention to your body, or checking your mind's thoughts? That may seem like a lot of effort for nothing. After all, not knowing your soul and its desires hasn't hurt you up to now. Why is it so important to listen to your soul?

Because this is "It" baby. This is the whole enchilada. It's all you've got. Your soul is the heart of your true self; without it, you would not exist. Someday your body will shrivel up like a raisin, your mind will get crusty like yesterday's toast, but your soul is yours eternally. It is the only real estate you will be taking with you when you leave here.

Because it is the heart of your true self, it holds the key to your happiness, success and good health. When you follow the direction of your soul's true compass, you will be led to all the good you deserve. When you live a more soul-filled life, you are led to do the things that are good for you and those close to you. In fact, you easily attract these things to you. There is no more need for violence, hunger, fear, jealousy, hate or war. Your soul does not need or want these things to thrive and complete itself.

Success, freedom, wisdom and happiness lie in how well you converse with your inner self. Your soul is waiting for you to wake up, say, "Yes!" and smell the roses. It is waiting for you to give up the struggle of fear, stop searching for an enemy around every corner, or believing in the devil (that's "lived" spelled backwards!), paranoia, lack or poverty. It is waiting for you to give up your belief that you are serving a life sentence here on Prison Earth and there is no way out.

You're thinking that this is not you. You didn't pick up this book to hear the same old stuff about "change your attitude, change your life." If a truly happy life can be attained by a simple change of attitude, then why is it so many people are still suffering? There has to be more to it than that. There has to be a better way—a more holistic approach—to changing your life.

Let me make it perfectly clear. When I say, "My Soul is *Me* and *Mine*," I am not referring to any particular religion, sect or creed. Growing your soul has nothing to do with cultural, ritual or mythological beliefs. This is personal. Your soul is *your* soul and no one has a claim on it but you. *Soul*, in this instance, is the core of your being, an intangible element that knows all about you and holds the mystery of why you are here.

What I have been laying out for you in each chapter is a process you can use to communicate truly with your soul and your soul's desire. All your life, your soul has been trying to give you a vision of your life. It has been sneaking little clues into every nook and cranny you pass along your journey. Sometimes you've paid attention, seized the moment and taken the right road. While other times, you've ignored what's been presented and learned the hard way what is good for you. Big whopping clues and minor indicators have shown up periodically throughout your life, but you may have been too busy struggling to have noticed.

Big Clues And Minor Indicators

Here are some of the big clues and small indictors for you to reflect on in your personal and professional life. Let's take a look at some you may be familiar with:

Minor Indicators

Your dominant color personality style is one of the minor indicators of your life purpose. (If you don't remember your dominant color personality styles, take a moment and go back to Chapter Two to refresh your memory.) Is your dominant personality style Blue, Green, Red or Yellow?

Remember that you have access to all four of these styles: Blues are relationship-oriented. Greens are project-oriented. Reds are goal-oriented. And Yellows are fun-oriented. So what has determined your dominant style? Is your particular style the result of parental or cultural influences or is it simply an organic, innate part of you?

I've come to believe it's a bit of both. Certainly parental, professional and cultural influences play a part, yet consider what you were attracted to as a child.

From the moment she could walk, our daughter Susan, organized our lives. At the age of one year, large glass ashtrays toddled and teetered above her head then landed thunderously in the kitchen sink. One day, while shopping for groceries, I discovered that she had made a mental list of the entire contents under my friend Marge's sinks.

As Susan grew older, I remember cleaning her room and hearing her complaining about me moving "all my stuff." Do I have to go on about how Green Susan is? Once I knew how a Green ticked I stopped trying to make her into something she was not. She is now an executive project manager for a major corporation—only fitting!

Think back to the times when you excelled at something. A teacher, parent, coworker or friend commented on your ability or skill. Perhaps you won an award, went the extra mile or did something extraordinary at the time. Something in your heart of hearts told you that this was something you would love to do if given the opportunity. But life happens, and the rational "you" either scoffed at the idea or thought it was too far out of your reach. You threw up limitations, like education, relationships, children, health issues, career, or finances.

Pushed to the corner, your soul was waving a big, honking, red flag saying, "Follow me." But you couldn't hear it. You were too busy struggling and fighting or calling yourself inadequate. What a waste of time and resources; all this time you could have been heading in the direction of your soul's desires and living a happy healthy life. Would have…could have. But it is never too late.

"Struggle however is not natural.
It is an unholy battle we fight with ourselves."
Stuart Wilde, *Life Was Never Meant to be a Struggle*

Other Minor Indicators

Minor indicators are subtle messages that bring on stress or leave you with an uneasy, nagging sense that aspects of your life are slightly off-center. You may notice:

- Job or career dissatisfaction
- Unhappy personal relationships
- Limited finances

- Guilty feelings about anything

- Low body energy

- Fear and doubt about self

Being slightly off-center isn't a big problem, but it can have noticeable effects. For example, imagine yourself walking around all the time with one leg shorter than the other. Your amazing body and mind will adapt to anything. Yet if you don't correct this predicament very soon your hips, back, thighs and head will ache. Your perception of life will be altered. A grumpy, depressed being that is not your true self, will appear.

If these so called little stresses on the body and mind continue, your heart and other vital, internal organs will be affected. It's at this point when what I call **Big Clues** will make themselves known.

Big Clues

Big clues are wake-up calls. Your soul has been trying to wake you up to your true self for years. Everything short of hitting you over the head has been tried. Unwilling to pay attention or reluctant to change, you are about to experience a force of nature. The nature of neglect manifests itself in numerous significant ways: divorce, loss of your job, bankruptcy, being arrested, cancer, heart failure, a near-death experience, among others.

These are all wake-up calls. You weren't standing on some street corner when they just happened to you. Your soul has been planting wake-up signs all along the way.

When you gave into your ego's belief in separateness and struggle, you told yourself that this is the way other people live, so it must be all right for me. But *is* it right for you? Are you happy with your life or is your soul still waiting for you to wake up?

The Benefits of Soulful Living

Read the following benefits, then ask yourself how each one would affect your life if you were to take action in that direction. Make a note of what action you will take to accomplish this and how it will feel.

🕱 Relieve Stress

Your soul wants you to do what you love doing. When you are engaged in the things you love doing, stress becomes a happy six-letter word, while time flies as you excel in your achievements. You relax into your purpose, you have a sense of where you are going and how much fun you are having. Oh, you'll face difficulties or challenges—the lessons of life. These will not bother you because you are doing the thing you love and, thereby, attracting more of the same into your life.

"Feel the power that comes from focusing on what excites you."

Action Notes: How will my stress level be affected if I do what you love doing? How can I incorporate more of what I love into my everyday life?

_____

_____

🕱 Stand Your Ground

True leadership is sensing what is right, then taking action to steer the situation in that direction. Your soul wants you to take charge, stand your ground, and live and love your life. Although the circumstances of your life at this moment may seem unchangeable, stand your ground, be persistent and ask for what you want. By increasing your ability to let people know who you are you, you become stronger and clearer about who you *believe* you are and what you want. Nothing will get in the way of what you want except your doubt and fear. Your soul knows no doubt or fear; it only knows your intention.

178

*"Sometimes it takes effort to discover that
life was meant to be effortless."*

Rust Berkus, *Appearances*

Action Notes: What will I risk? And what do I see happening
when I stand up for what I want?

_____

_____

☼ Grow Compassion

You empathize with a father who has lost his job, a rape victim,
or the people who suffer and continue to suffer after the New Orleans
storm, Katrina. But what about the reviled senator in the midst of a sex
scandal, the rapist, the murderer or the inept federal authorities who
failed to alleviate suffering? Do you say, "Well, that's another story...
they did something despicable"?

Compassion is for everyone. Jesus did not say, "Okay, you good
people with smaller problems go stand over there, and you people
who've made **big** mistakes... well, forget you." Compassion comes
from your heart and soul, where you *absolutely know* oneness with all
things. As you practice connecting with your soul's desires, you will
grow more compassionate toward yourself and others.

*Her little girl was late arriving home from school,
so the mother began to scold her daughter,
but stopped and asked, "Why are you so late?"
"I had to help another girl. She was in trouble,"
replied her daughter.
"What did you do to help her?"
"Oh, I sat down and helped her cry."*

Anonymous

179

Action Notes: Who in my life needs my compassion? How would this be helpful to me?

_____

_____

⚇ Make A Difference in The World

When you're caught up in the everyday worries and mêlées of life, it is not easy see where and how your energy and soul purpose can make a difference in the world. However, when you are living a soul-filled life, your "laser beam" thoughts and actions inevitably affect the world around you, extending out to a world of people you will never meet.

When you trust your true self and communicate from soul's desires, you are most powerful. Your presence is felt without you saying a word and you can move mountains by your intentions. This is how the great leaders like Mother Teresa, Mahatma Gandhi, Nelson Mandela and others succeeded in bringing social, political and moral change to the world around them. Their thoughts and actions were soul based.

"The one thing in the world of value is the active soul."
Ralph Waldo Emerson

Action Notes: What would my life be like if I trusted and expressed my true self?

_____

_____

⚇ Point Your Compass in The True Direction

As you practice body, mind and spiritual awareness, your soul's vision of your life will be revealed to you. It is then that you will have tapped into the all-knowing part of you which, like a compass, will lead you in the right direction. There is a price to pay to find your true purpose in life. It will cost you the pain of giving up the concept that you are caught in the crossfire. You'll have to abandon the mantras of "life is hard" and "stuff just happens to me." You will have to take charge of your life. You will have to listen to what your soul desires for you, and take action.

We will be discussing more about soul desires and how to point your compass toward your soul's vision in a later chapter.

> *"It matters not how strait the gate,*
> *How charged with punishments the scrolls,*
> *I am the master of my fate: I am the captain of my soul."*
> W.C. Henley, *Invictus*

Action Notes: In what areas of my life do I feel I am in control?

_____

_____

ஃ Suffer No Fools

You will no longer have a need for drama or fear; you will no longer have to fight an enemy. You will be free from suffering fools. Dabbling in gossip, walking around wounded, limiting your risks—all these will bore you. You will regard the drama of everyday life with the same interest as you would a Shakespearian play.

> *"All the world's a stage,*
> *And all the men and women merely players.*
> *They have their exits and their entrances,*
> *And one man in his time plays many parts,*
> *His acts being seven ages."*
> William Shakespeare, *As You Like It*

Your life will be filled with fun, light, easy things that give you great enjoyment and bring others the same. In some cases, you will make new friends and the dynamics of your life will change, but when all is said and done you will rise to the top like so much county cream.

Action Notes: How would my life be affected if I no longer suffered fools with gossip, fear, or worry?

_____

_____

⚷ Access The Healer Within

When you think of healers, you're probably not including yourself in this realm. However, if you stop to think about it, anyone who has ever recovered from an illness or injury healed herself or himself. Others may have participated in the healing process but ultimately the healer within is responsible.

An evangelical preacher who laid hands upon you may have facilitated your healing, but _you_ are the one who decided to reach out and connect with your inner Spirit. You may therefore believe that Jesus, Mohammad, Blessed Mary, Buddha, Shiva or a Mayan God, healed you and they did—but not without your permission.

What is important to remember is that you have the power within you to heal yourself and others from anything at anytime. Deciding to access this power and to utilize the good of all things is the act of saying "YES!" to life.

Action Notes: What are my feelings and thoughts about healers and my own ability to heal myself and others?

_____

_____

"The only way to find the limits of the possible is by going beyond them to the impossible."
Arthur C. Clarke

Your soul yearns for you to wake up and live a soul-based life. Every day you touch people's lives with your soul, intentionally or unintentionally. What if you were to intentionally live your life guided by your soul or heart? What if you were to express loving actions and words from your true self? How different the world would be if we communicated soul to soul with ourselves and others. Our compassion level would go through the roof, our capacity to heal ourselves and others would be phenomenal. There is no end to the possibilities that lie in store for those of us who are willing to say "YES!" to a soul-filled life. The following story demonstrates two different types of healing: a physical healing and the healing that comes from being curious and open to whatever Spirit reveals to you in the moment.

The Healing Power of a 'Blonde Weekend'

"The true adventurer goes forth aimless and uncalculating to meet and greet an unknown fate."
O. Henry

Carrie, my daughter-in-law, is six degrees left of center. This is not a bad thing; however she's not your typical woman by any stretch of the imagination. Her magnetic gyro compass has a flair for the bizarre and downright wacky—and somehow this endures her to me. Carrie has what I call a "blonde mind." She thinks way, way, *way* outside the box, any box. She lives life lightly and changes her hair color as often as her mind. This is the kind of person you want to have plan your next vacation, or "blonde weekend", because there *is* no plan.

One day she announced that she was taking me to a health spa for my birthday. I was thrilled. I envisioned a picturesque sun rising over wisteria-draped lattice beside a crystal blue spa. I could just imagine José, my personal masseuse, pampering and steaming me until I was done.

"Let's get away from it all, Mom," Carrie bounced. "Think of it as a Blonde Weekend"

Just east of Salem, nestled in ancient cedars and firs is Oregon's Breitenbush Hot Springs. Since the 1930's people from around the world have come to take a dip in its 108° waters. The setting is straight out of the movie *A River Runs Through It*. Sheer rock cliffs formed a mossy, fern-studded backdrop for a meadow of steaming pools, edged by the roaring Breitenbush River. This is a place to rest and unwind mind, body and Spirit.

This rustic wonderland may not have been the spa of my dreams, but in many ways it was better. The aroma of the forest floor, the clean crisp air and the quiet surroundings instantly soothed my soul. After checking, in we headed toward the serene meadow of rising vapors and wooden benches. As we approached, I noticed a pile of clothing, socks and shoes. It suddenly struck me: these people are *naked*! I had never been to Breitenbush before, never skinny dipped in the woods before and—well, certainly not totally naked.

Willing to try almost anything once, I disrobed and began my dunk. I surrendered in an instant and thoroughly enjoyed the experience. Just for a moment, however, I did have the urge to take Carrie by her tie-dyed lapel and shout, "WHAT WERE YOU THINKING?" But that's what a blonde weekend is all about, venturing into the unknown, trying something different, and discovering new things about your-self.

After we'd been soaking like two Lipton Flow-Thru Tea Bags, Carrie finally sighed, "I think we'd better get out before our bones cook." All I could manage in the mist of my fatigue was a nod of my head. My rump roast was done. Gripping the side of the pool, we slithered our half-cooked flesh to the pine bench and melted into mere puddles of our former selves. We found our legs and slid them one at a time into our jeans. Then we rested ten minutes.

A gourmet vegetarian buffet, served at the lodge, revived us from the dead. With our stomachs full, we became giddy. Like happy drunks we followed the winding path to cabin B-4. "Before what?" Carrie quipped and giggled.

The wooden door to the outhouse-shaped-cabin creaked open: revealing two bunks, a rag rug and a well-worn plank floor. No brochure could have—or would have—mentioned these amenities.

We rolled sleeping bags out onto pristine white sheet-covered-mattresses and collapsed. Like two teenagers on a sleepover, time slipped away. We told raunchy jokes and laughed until we nearly peed our pants. We were high on life, enjoying the moment. Worries disappeared and we found ourselves in what the Buddhist call the *nothingness zone*. With relaxed bodies and empty minds, our eyelids gradually closed.

A moan from across the room startled me—or was I dreaming? "Mmmmmooommmm... are you awake?" Maybe if I lie perfectly still... she'll think I'm asleep. (This worked when I was raising children.)

"Mmmmmmooommmm... are you awake?" came the whimper again.

Do I look awake? I thought, as I groped for the clock that read 2:30! Did I forget to turn off the "OPEN 24 HRS." neon sign on my "mom" forehead? What part of this picture says I'm *awake*? But I rubbed my eyes and replied, "I am now... what's wrong?" (As if I wanted to know.)

Please don't think badly of me. You must understand that my children are alive today by the grace of God. Their ability to sleep through the night as infants saved them from an uncertain fate. I remember how annoyed I was when my son woke me at 2:00 AM simply because he couldn't suck milk out of a shoe lace. Don't ask! The point is, my compassion meter is on zero in the wee hours; all I wanted to do was sleep.

"I'm, sorry to wake you." Carrie muttered, "I have an awful headache... I think I got overheated. I feel really bad... my ears are ringing... my shoulders hurt... do you have any Ibuprofen"?

Staggering to the end of my bunk I rummage through my luggage dazed and incoherent. I was desperate for a pill, any pill. If I'd have found baby aspirin, estrogen or a lint-covered birth control pill, I'd have given it to her.

"Carrie, I don't have any pills." I turned toward the shadowy figure in the next bed, no answer. Had she fallen back to sleep?

Inches from the pillow I heard, "Could you rub my neck for a few minutes... maybe it will help?"

In the darkness, stumbling across the room I found her shoulders as hard as the river rock we'd tripped on earlier. Trying to sleep and massage at the same time didn't really work. I finally became lucid enough to realize that she was truly in pain. She needed me to do something, but what?

Still in the alpha state of sleep I began to take in deep, centering breaths while asking God what I should do. Stretching and straightening my spine I felt the presence of Ki energy; a sense Oneness and calmness of Spirit came over me. Envisioning a golden light pouring out of my hands and into Carrie seemed to invite me to have no question as to whether this would work on not. That didn't seem important. All I needed to do was allow Spirit to guide me.

"Carrie, take a deep breath," I began softly, "now let it out. And another deep breath and let go, relax. Imagine a pinpoint of golden light moving to wherever the pain is right now. Let that light grow larger and larger."

"Do you sense the light, Carrie?"

"Yes, Mom, I do..." she whispered.

"Golden liquid light of love energy is pouring over you, through the top of your head… down your shoulders, and slowly moving out your toes." Taking another breath we continued to stay with that vision until there was a sense that our Spirits had become one. When it was time to stop I did.

In the soft cotton of my pillow as I heard, "Thanks…Mom."

Morning broke through the homemade curtains. Torn between sleep and marvel, I rustled for clothes as Carrie burrowed in and said, "I'm fine, see you at breakfast."

The crisp air bit at my cheeks as I made my way to a little octagonal chapel situated in a stand of firs. A stained glass panel centered the room and clear windows on each side opened to a view of the river below. Collecting one of the cushions that lined the walls I settled in to observe tiny snowflakes falling on darkened winter leaves while the river roared on.

An old Peggy Lee song ran through my mind, *Is That All There Is?* Yes, that is all there is to life, Judy. What's here in this moment is all there is to life. The compelling peace I'd experienced, the previous night, was like none I had experienced before. It was the first time I had truly heard what my soul was saying; this is what you're here to do, this is the vehicle you will use to make a difference in the world.

> *"I had no hesitancy about becoming God's messenger because*
> *I was simply becoming who I really am."*
>
> Neale Donald Walsch

Isn't it time you gave yourself a Blonde Weekend? Take time to connect with nature and the nature of your soul. You have within you a soul ready to express it's true self and be a communicating healer. Isn't about time you said "YES!?"

Resource Center

✿ *Make A Difference with The Power of Compassion,* by Mary Robinson Reynolds and Elizabeth Silance Ballard. This is a poignant story about a little boy who was behaving badly in school, and failing by fifth grade. It is also about a teacher who, by her willlingness to change her perspective, gained compassion and understanding, which made a difference in Teddy's life and the lives he consequently touched.

This is a story that bypasses the head and goes straight to the heart. It is a positive reminder of how we can turn a life around completely, with the power of compassion.

✿ *Power vs. Force: The Hidden Determinants of Human Behavior,* by David R. Hawkins, M.D, Ph.D. examines the power of thoughts as energy. My favorite quote:

"Individuals of great power throughout human history have been those who have totally aligned themselves with powerful attractors. Again and again, they have stated that the power they manifested was not of themselves. Each has attributed the source of the power to something greater than themselves."

✿ *Seat of the Soul,* by Gary Zukav provides a new perspective and approach to living a soul-based life. My favorite quote:

"You may seek companionship and warmth for example but if your unconscious intention is to keep people at a distance the experience of separation and pain will surface again and again until you come to understand that you, yourself are creating them. Eventually, you will draw to you the highest-frequency currents that each situation has to offer. Eventually, you will come to understand that love heals everything, and love is all there is."

❧ *The Art of Happiness: A Handbook for Living,*
by Dalai Lama helped me to understand that the very
purpose of our lives is to seek happiness; no matter whether
one believes in this religion or that. My favorite quote:

*"The ability to shift perspective, the capacity to view one's
problems "from different angles," is nurtured by a supple quality
of mind. The ultimate benefit of a supple mind is that it allows us
to embrace all of life---to be fully alive and human."*

**❧ *The Self-Aware Universe: How Consciousness Creates
the Material World*,** by Amit Goswami, Ph. D.

*"Without the immanent world of manifestation, there would
be no soul, no self that experiences itself as separate from the
objects it perceives."*

**❧ *Quantum Healing: Exploring the Frontiers of Mind/Body
Medicine*,** by Deepak Chopra, M.D. explores the deepest
core of the mind-body system. This core is where healing
begins. My favorite quote:

*"Nothing I have said so far about the body's know-how
is hypothetical. We have all been informed, doctors and
public alike, about the body's wondrous intricacy.
Yet we persist in thinking of the body as an obsolete mold,
as basically matter, but with a smart technician
inside who moves the matter around.
This technician was once called the soul; now it tends
to be demoted to a ghost inside the machine."*

❧ Media Resources, websites you may want to explore:

- www.experiencefestival.com
- www.quantumquest.com
- www.soulslight.com

Ki Exercise # 9

Now it is your turn to experience a deeper connection with your body, mind and soul, and thereby be truly able to make a significant difference in the world. Sit straight, in a comfortable position and close your eyes. Breathe in the energy of the moment. Breathe out all your cares. Let your mind be centered once again on your palms. Clap your hands together ten times. Now rub them together briskly and steadily.

Place your hands in front of your chest, palms facing each other. Focus your attention on your palms. There is energy in every part of your body: your head, neck, heart, stomach, intestines, muscles, hands and feet. Your hands are an extension of your soul or Spirit's energy. There is no need for thinking. Let your mind be empty. This is your time to experience, accept and love your energy.

Imagine a light of connective energy between your hands. Focus on this energy for a moment. Let it grow warmer and stronger as you move your hands in and out. Let your mind go. Let yourself relax into the moment. Feel the energy and power that is yours. This is your energy to use as you wish. This is the energy within you that will help you make a difference in the world.

Move your hands together and farther apart and back together again. Feel the sensation of light energy in your hands. You may be in wonder or awe the first time you experience this. However as you practice feeling this Ki exercise daily you will soon appreciate and become accustomed to the presence of your energy and how you may be able to utilize it for the greater good. Breathe in energy, breathe out energy.

This Ki exercise will change your life and therefore change the world around you. Accept your inner energy and SAY "YES! TO LIFE NOW!

Chapter 10

The Power Matrix to A "Yes!" Life

*"People create their own questions because they are afraid
to look straight. All you have to do is look straight
and see the road and when you see it,
don't sit looking at it—walk."*

Ayn Rand

How exciting! Now you know what your soul's purpose is, you're ready to go out into the world and truly make it difference. Right? No? I would have thought the last chapter would have cinched it for you. [She smiles here!] Just keep in mind that life is a practice. Nothing worthwhile comes easy and we are practicing life so we can live life well.

In this practice, please be kind to yourself as you move through the process of change. Life isn't a race with a grand prize at the end. In fact, your only reward will be to die peacefully knowing that in your own unique way you did your best to make a difference in the world.

You may intellectually understand the concepts that I have introduced in the last few chapters. However, to really make a difference, you must be smart and learn to practice and grow your abilities. Trust me—you are smart enough to change your life. Your intellect is not in question. What's important is your ability to connect and communicate with your body, mind and Spirit. So this chapter is dedicated to helping you make this unquestionably vital connection.

When I talk about this essential link, let me emphasize that there is nothing more important in this world than your ability to connect deeply with who you really are and to live life authentically. Nothing. Everything else pales in comparison. Everything you say and do has a visceral affect on you and the world around you. But you already know that—intellectually—there's no doubt about it. Now it's time for you to *know* this from your toes up, deeply and unequivocally, so that you lead your life with the strength of an unconquerable Spirit.

What Is Your Soul's Purpose?

You are not your body; you are not your mind. You are, solely, your soul. So stop fussing over the small stuff. Stop letting circumstances, conditions and issues detour you from what you know is good for you. So what is your soul's purpose? Even a rock has a purpose. Each of us came here do something. I can't begin to know what that might be for you, I'm still working on my own unfolding journey and that's quite enough to keep me busy, thank you.

However, what I have discovered is that you do not have to become something, reach some exalted height of excellence, or be saved. You don't have to wait until you lose weight, stop smoking or give up sex to have a happier, healthier life. And listen to this: you don't even have to know specifically what your soul desires for you. That's right. And *thank God!* The thing is, your soul already knows; it's just a matter of you listening and letting yourself be soulfully guided.

These honorable intentions may assist you on your journey toward a clearer understanding of yourself, but they will not stand alone as the answer to finding the peace you long for and deserve.

The fact is when you say "Yes!" to life, your life will unfold in such a way that you will grow to appreciate and cherish your unique, extraordinary perceptions of life. Through your practice, your soul's purpose will be revealed and you will no longer feel the need to fight against anything. A war on drugs, a war on crime, a war on terror, a war on cancer, a war on violence or a war against another country or its people will not be obligatory. You will recognize the principle of Universal Law that says: What you fight against pushes back a hundredfold. Therefore it doesn't make sense to live any other way than in peace. Your purpose is peace.

If you've failed at dieting, loathe exercise, smoke like a chimney, have unhealthy relationships, can't stand your relatives, or your career is something less than you aspire it to be, listen up. There is good news. The good news is you decided to say "Yes!" to life the moment you began reading this book. It doesn't matter what your life is like at this moment, because in the next moment it is going to change. So why not be the master of this change and practice using your instruments (body, mind and Spirit) to design your life the way you want it to be?

Three Things You'll Accomplish with The Power Matrix

The Power Matrix is designed to help you become the designer and master of your life's journey. It is a way of practicing and processing the changes you would like to see happen and therefore enable you to be the healthy communicator and healer for yourself and others. The result of this practice will be a soul-based life. The benefits embedded into the practice will help you accomplish three things:

⚘ ONE: LOVE YOUR BODY

I don't mean *like* your body, I mean **love** your body passionately and completely, just the way it is right now. As you practice this you will discover the profound, multi-layered connection your body has with your soul's desires. These are just a few of a myriad of benefits:

- You increase your compassion, appreciation and awareness of this magnificent instrument you call your body.

- You are able to assist others in healing themselves without putting any stress or strain on yourself.

- You take charge of your life and with a clear-minded laser-focus are able to accomplish things you have only dreamed of.

- You realize that *your body is not you, but yours*; a rented, superlative lump of flesh that has been borrowed from a higher power with the expectations of wonderful things.

- You are able to intuitively sense body energy in yourself and other people and thereby be able to communicate more clearly and effectively.

- You create a sound and formidable communication with your body so that you are able to identify any malaise or dis-ease and take appropriate action to reverse it.

- You attract to you the good you desire and deserve because of your willingness to Love your body completely.

"I am so absorbed in the wonder of earth and the life upon it that I cannot think of heaven and the angels. I have enough for this life."
Pearl S. Buck

✿ TWO: LOVE YOUR MIND

I don't mean *like* your mind a little. I mean *love* and appreciate your mind as the wonderful amazing instrument that has been entrusted to you. Through your efforts, you will realize the effect your thoughts have on your life. Clear down to the cellular level, you will use your creative mind to live and love life. Here are some of the benefits of mind awareness:

- You—clearly and with precision—use the power of your mind to attract goodness into your life.

- You discover that the differences between people are really the glue that holds all of us all together.

- You strengthen and balance your mind so that decision-making comes quickly and easily.

- You recognize that you are the leader of your life and the leader for others to follow in a gentle and loving way.

- You become a source of wisdom and pride that will assist others in their search for service and meaning.

- You increasingly unveil your soul's path more clearly and therefore live a soul-based life.

- You have a powerful presence that will serve you well in any profession, relationship or financial decision.

> *"I finally figured out that the only reason*
> *to be alive is to enjoy it."*
>
> Rita Mae Brown

❧ THREE: LOVE YOUR SOUL

I don't mean *like* the idea that you have a soul. I mean **love** and trust your soul's desires with a sense of knowing that goes beyond all reasoning or logical understanding. Let yourself be guided by the invisible force of nature. Here are a few of the benefits of a soul-based life:

- You create an indestructible faith in a higher power that is innately yours.

- You effortlessly and deeply connect with your soul's desires on a daily, hourly, minute-by-second basis.

- You authentically communicate who you are and what you want, with love and compassion for others.

- You dissolve issues promptly, because you know the truth

about the dramas and fears that can stifle life force.

- You discover the magnificent and all-consuming love, peace, oneness, joy and bliss that living a soul-based life earns.

- You realize that life is an adventurous journey of changes, challenges and choices; it flows as easily as you choose it to.

- You learn that a soul-based life is a quickened life; what took years or months to resolve can be settled in hours or seconds.

"Many people have a wrong idea of what constitutes true happiness. It is not attained through self-gratification but through fidelity to a worthy purpose."

Helen Keller

The Power Matrix to a "Yes!" Life

Let me make perfectly clear that a soul-based "Yes!" life doesn't preclude you from experiencing pain, or from feeling lousy or depressed. No one gets out of this life without some suffering that, I hope, wakes you and gives you the opportunity to appreciate that you are alive. This is the only thing that pain is good for. The practice of a soul-based life does, however, increase your experience of gratitude, joy and ultimate bliss. That's why it's so important for you to experience and practice what I am about to share with you.

"A balance between an individual's coping skills and his or her stress level can also be the tipping point of whether one is more susceptible to illness or not," said Oakley Ray, Ph. D., of the Department of Psychology and Psychiatry at Vanderbilt University. He went on to say, "According to the literature, coping skills can be defined as having a good knowledge of the world you live in; having inner resources and believing you have some control over life events; having social support which is proven to have a direct affect on mortality rate; and having a spiritual orientation to oneself and the world."

The **Power Matrix**, which I will share with you, is a two-part tool that helps you improve your ability to communicate with yourself and with those around you. First, the **Power Matrix Questionnaire** will assist you in discovering the many indicators and clues that your soul has been communicating to you through your life experiences. You will gain consensus and an understanding of the direction your life will take if you are led by your soul's desires.

The **Power Matrix Color Visualization Meditations** are designed to help you connect with the four different color personality styles and thereby assist you in connecting with your body and mind so you will improve your coping skills, lower your stress level and create a deeper understanding of yourself and others.

These two exercises will help you gain confidence in your ability to listen and talk to your body on an energetic level and facilitate your ability to communicate more clearly with yourself and others.

Take a deep breath and relax. Be honest with yourself, without making yourself right or wrong, as you answer the following questions:

Power Matrix Questionnaire

As I look at my physical characteristics in the mirror, what do I see?

_____

_____

What I've been told about me:

_____

_____

What I tell myself about me:

_____

_____

What I really know about me:

_____

_____

How do I feel about my life so far?

_____

_____

How old do I feel? _____

What do I think about my life currently?

_____

_____

How would I change my life?

_____

_____

How would I change others?

_____

_____

Here are three things that I appreciate most about myself:

_____

_____

If money were no object, where would I go? With whom would I go? What would I do?

_____

_____

Imagining the ideal "ME"—how would he or she look?

_____

_____

What qualities would the ideal "ME" have?

_____

_____

How is she/he different from me now?

_____

_____

What would I have to give up to become my ideal self?

_____

_____

What are my strengths?

_____

_____

This is one of my weaknesses:

_____

Here are three dominant characteristics of someone I dislike:

_____

_____

Here are three major characteristics of someone I admire:

_____

_____

This book, song or movie best describes my life:

_____

What would I title a book, song or movie about my life?

_____

What am I like when I'm alone?

_____

_____

What am I like when I get what I want?

_____

_____

What am I like when I don't get what I want?

_____

_____

Here are ten things that are most important to me:

1. _____   6. _____

2. _____   7. _____

3. _____   8. _____

4. _____   9. _____

5. _____   10. _____

Where do I want to be in five years, physically, financially, spiritually?

_____

_____

Chapter 10 : The Power Matrix to A "Yes!" Life

What am I now doing that will lead me in that direction?

_____

_____

What am I doing that will keep me from accomplishing it?

_____

_____

What types of people, places or things inspire me?

_____

_____

How would I describe my Spiritual life on a scale of one to ten (ten being the most active)? _____

What do I do for fun?

_____

_____

Thank yourself for taking the time to look honestly at YOU. Breathe in... breathe out. Let go, let your mind relax for a moment.

Now, Search For Your Soul's Purpose

Read over your answers thoughtfully. Look for the indicators and markers that your soul has been trying to show you about your purpose. Now let's apply this information to your search for your soul's purpose:

What unique qualities did I discover about myself?

_____

_____

What patterns or indicators are prevalent in my life?

_____

_____

What role do these indicators play out in my professional and personal life choices today?

_____

_____

What do I believe has been the message of my soul's desire?

_____

_____

What am I willing to do to fulfill it?

_____

_____

This exercise may or may not help you sort out your soul's desire. Unfortunately—or perhaps, fortunately—there are no scientific, systematic, controlled studies to give you the answers you seek. I can tell you, nonetheless, that this has worked for me for over twenty years because it is a simple process and I have a very simple mind. You attract to you what you practice.

Here's How I Answered The Last Question...

Of course, there are no "right" or "wrong" answers and while everyone will respond differently, you may be interested in what others have said. So I'll share my final answer with you:

"What am I willing to do to fulfill it? To live consciously and courageously, to resonate with love and compassion, to awaken the great spirits within myself and others, and to one day leave this world more peaceful than I came."

202

The Power Matrix of the Colors

The four distinct color personality styles within you hold the key to increasing your understanding of your soul. By gradually balancing and incorporating each style into your daily communication practice you will expand your understanding of true Oneness. By *Oneness*, I mean; your ability to appreciate not only the commonalities that draw us together, but the distinct, fundamental differences of each individual that actually are the glue that binds us enduringly to each other.

Each of the following visualizations was devised for a specific color personality style. However because you are made up of all four of these personality styles, I recommend that you utilize each visualization-meditation. It is important that you *practice* this exercise to get the most effective results. You may want to read these visualizations out loud and record them in your own voice; then play them back in the morning before rising and in the evening before retiring.

Warm up: Before you begin, take a moment to do the *Hoe Down Slap Down*: Cup your right hand and begin by tapping your left shoulder firmly, thirty times. Now cup your left hand and tap your right shoulder firmly, thirty times. Now tap your chest, stomach, ribs, lower abdomen and hips, fifty times each. Breathe in and breathe out.

✄ Visualization Meditation: *Blue*

Close your eyes and draw in a deep breath. Let it go and relax your body completely. Straighten your spine as you sit comfortably in a quiet space. Focus on your body; let your mind relax so your soul can comfort you.

Imagine yourself walking along a path in the forest. You see before you a clear blue sky; you smell the warm earth and feel a gentle breeze as it rustles the trees. As you walk along, your senses are enlivened as you suddenly become aware of the beauty and wholeness of your surroundings. Your body breathes in the magnificence of the moment.

At first you are overwhelmed by the energy and sense of strength of this special place.

Yet very soon you become accustomed to its power and decide to sit down, rest your body and drink it in. As you breathe in the moment; you lean back against a giant tree. Each breath takes you deeper…and deeper…and deeper, as you melt deeper into the tree. Very soon, you are one with the wisdom of the tree. Your body is the body of the tree. You feel the divine harmony, strength and wisdom within you. You can sense the innate intelligence that knows how to grow, knows how to sway with the energy around it, knows how to abundantly procreate and, best of all, knows how to heal itself.

You smile at the feeling of Oneness in the moment. There is no room for fear, doubt, guilt or anger. There is only a sense of peaceful wholeness. Your body has within it the same intelligence as every living thing. It knows how to serve you. It knows everything.

As there is a core in the center of the tree, there is a core within the center of your body. This core is the true strength of your body and your soul. It is the center of everything you experience.

Take a moment now to focus on your chakras and the energy core that connects each of them to the other. Feel the energy and power and its relationship to all things. Become aware of your chakra energy centers. Bring your mind to the base of the spine and focus on chakra number one—a glowing red, sexual energy chakra. This is where all life energy is created; this is where passion is generated to your entire body. Relationships are deepened and nurtured here. Let the warmth of this chakra permeate your entire body, allowing you to easily create warm, loving and balanced relationships.

You love relationships. Loving relationships feed your soul and give you great satisfaction. You love your body and gratefully give it anything it needs to help you create healthy loving relationships. Let your mind now move upward to another important relationship chakra—chakra number five, your throat chakra. Focus all your attention on your throat chakra. Imagine the whole area relaxing with the loving energy you are sending it now. Imagine the muscles around your throat and neck becoming calm and supple. Take a moment to forgive anyone you may feel has offended you. As you forgive others, you create compassion in your heart. Your ability to communicate easily and effortlessly with others grows. You are free to convey your true desires and feelings in appropriate ways.

If there is discomfort anywhere in your body—even the slightest pain—now would be a good time to send loving energy to the area. You can communicate with your body anywhere, anytime to give you courage and strength to accomplish great things. Breathe in and out and slowly open your eyes.

⚘ Visualization Meditation: *Green*

Take a deep breath and let it out. Close your eyes, let go of your thoughts and relax your body. Find your favorite quiet space and breathe. This is your time. Adjust your body so that your spine is straight and your chin is slightly down. This is your time to take care and love you.

Imagine yourself happily walking along a quiet trail somewhere in nature. The sky is clear, the air is warm and a slight breeze soothes your skin. As you breathe in the beauty around you, you are inspired by the Oneness and calmness of life. Breathe in and notice that everything around you is in perfect order just the way it is. All that you are experiencing right now is in perfect order.

Your body and mind breathe in the splendor of the moment. You are humbled and awed by the sense of Oneness that you feel with all humanity, with all forms of life. Smile and let your mind accept this Oneness as the true reality, because you know on so many levels that the source of all is in all. Breathe in, breathe out. Stay present in the moment. Feel the Oneness of your breath, feel the Oneness within your body. You have a sense of completeness in the nothingness of this moment.

As you walk along the trail you come to a clearing, where off to one side you see a small grassy, green knoll. Drawing closer, you see stepping stones before you that lead upward to the top of the knoll. As you step onto the first stone, you observe a brilliant white light that illuminates the heavens. Each step you take draws you closer to the white light of pure love. You now open your arms wide and let the white light permeate every organ and every cell of your body. Tell yourself, I love my body... I love my beautiful body. Drink in this moment let it take you over.

As you let go you feel an innate strength and power within you. The white light of love is now a focused beam of light, directed straight at your heart chakra in the center of your chest. A warm glow of loving compassion opens your heart. Let your heart open and open. Breathe in the white light of love. Let it align with the center of your being, at your very core. This core is your connection to your soul. It is at the center of everything you do and say. In this moment your soul is speaking. What is it saying to you?

Breathe in and listen... let the love you feel in this moment radiate throughout your body. Let it move slowly upward through each chakra until it reaches the chakra at the top of your head. This chakra, in the cosmic energy realm, is vibrating in violet light. The Universal energy of pure LOVE surrounds you. Every endeavor or project that you undertake is easily and effortlessly completed now, because you invite this love energy into every aspect of your life.

Take a deep breath and listen to your body. What is it saying to you? If there is discomfort anywhere in your body—even the slightest pain—now is the time to send loving energy to this area. Let the light of love communicate your love and appreciation for your body. Breathe in and out gently and slowly open your eyes.

✿ Visualization Meditation: *Red*

Find a comfortable, quiet place. Breathe in this moment. This is your moment to let go and relax. Close your eyes and empty your thoughts. Breathe in, adjust your body so that your spine is straight and your chin is slightly down. Exhale. You have nowhere to go, there are no goals to reach. It is time for you to just relax and enjoy yourself.

Imagine in your mind's eye that you are seated on a park bench, relaxing in the warmth of a beautiful sunny day. From your bench you have an exquisite, panoramic view of the green meadow below. There is a small stream that etches slowly through shades and shadows of brilliant emerald. The earthy smell of moist soil and the energy of life in the moment are all around you. As you breathe in the beauty around you, you are inspired by the oneness and calmness of life. You notice that everything in nature has found its own completeness and order. Savor this feeling of completeness and let it go all the way to your toes.

Take a deep breath and let it out. Smile as you feel your body refresh and relax. Be present in the moment and know that everything is complete and whole in your life. Let go of preconceived ideas of how things should be and allow your inner self to be guided and loved.

Now bring your mind to your third chakra, located just below your navel. This is your connection with your abdominal brain where you carry your emotions and make decisions. This is your strength. You know how to make sound decisions, because they always come from this chakra energy. Let this chakra's yellow glow of divine wisdom and awareness permeate your body and mind. Let this loving energy fill every organ, every pore and every cell.

What does your soul desire of you? Let your mind stay here for awhile…. Breathe.

Use your mind to scan your body for any discomfort or even the slightest pain. If there is a part of your body that needs your attention, now is the time to send it loving, healing energy. You can communicate with your body anytime, anywhere because you love your body unconditionally. Breathe in and out and slowly open your eyes.

⚅ Visualization Meditation: *Yellow*

Let your mind relax. Let your body go. Breathe in… breathe out. Get into a comfortable position in a quiet area where you can be alone with your thoughts. Straighten your spine, curl in your tail bone and tuck your chin in slightly. Feel yourself begin to connect with the cosmic energy of life. Close your eyes and take in a deep breath. Let it go and relax your body completely.

Imagine yourself strolling along a garden path on a bright and peaceful day. Above you a crystal clear sky seems to dance against the dark green trees, while earthly smells and sounds fill your senses. Aliveness fills the air and inspires you to open your heart, mind and soul to its beauty. Breathe in the wonder of this moment and become one with the surroundings.

Off to one side, you notice a little pond nestled in a small clearing. You come to the edge of the pond to gaze into the crystal clear water. At first there's a fuzzy image in the water, but the longer you focus, the clearer the image becomes. It is a beautiful reflection of you. Your mind is transfixed on every detail, every attribute and every amazing feature of this image. There is loving energy radiating and glimmering from this reflection, rippling across the water and connecting to your inner self.

Soon you become One with the water and the loving energy of this image. You are the love you give and receive. You are One with your inner divine self. You are in touch with the innate intelligence that knows everything and is the source of all things. It knows how to love, how to forgive and how to attract good. Best of all, it knows how to heal your body and mind.

You smile as you feel the Oneness of the moment. Your mind now focuses on your heart chakra, at the center of your chest. A radiating green glow permeates your body and mind, filling every part of your being with love. Your love for yourself has opened your heart and has eliminated fear, doubt, guilt or anger. In the core of your body, you are filled with a sense of peaceful wholeness.

Happiness and joy are very important to you. You live your life seeking out moments of joy that bring happiness to yourself and others around you. As you drink in self love you increase your capacity to love unconditionally, and compassion grows in your heart. Breathe into your heart with love, and joy.

Fully relax your entire body. Imagine universal light energy coming from the chakra at the top of your head. From this cosmic realm, healing energy softly pours down over your head, shoulders, arms, torso, legs, thighs and out through your feet. Any discomfort or tenseness your body has been experiencing is soothed and healed now. Breathe in and out and slowly open your eyes.

To Derive The Greatest Benefit...

Remember that to get the most out of these visualization-meditations please integrate them into your daily practice. Trying something once may help you derive some benefit, but consistency, regularity and determination create permanent and long-lasting changes.

Resource Center

🔅 *Minding the Body, Mending the Mind*, by Joan Borysenko, Ph. D. shows you how to take control of you own physical and emotional well being. My favorite quote:

*"Mindfulness is meditation in action and involves a
'be here now' approach that allows life to unfold
without the limitation of prejudgment."*

Ki Exercise # 10

Get in as comfortable a position as possible. This could be lying down, sitting in a comfortable chair or in a yoga lotus position. Fully relax your entire body. Then take your consciousness inside your body, as you fully and slowly scan everywhere inside your skin. Be aware of areas which feel tense or even painful. Allow a few moments to experience the physical sensations in each of the areas. Then focus on the one that seems to call out most for attention.

Breathe into the pain and let your loving thoughts calm and sooth your entire body. Focus your attention on the physical sensation in all its nuances and observe how it changes.

Send nurturing energy in the form of words or phrases, like a parent would soothe a child. Tell yourself, "I see you, I feel you, I bless you, and I love you." It's okay if your mind wonders; just gently bring it back to focusing on the peace you are creating in your body, mind and Spirit. Breathe in. Breathe out.

Notice how your entire body has changed, because you chose to *let it change*. You are One with your magnificent body, your powerful mind and your unconquerable Spirit. Let go and let life unfold perfectly.

Chapter 11

You've Got to Be Crazy to Say "Yes!" to Life

"Live, live, live! Life is a banquet
and some poor suckers are starving to death."

Auntie Mame

*A*untie Mame is my hero. As a fictional character in Patrick Dennis's, 1955 novel and the 1958 movie starring Rosalind Russell, (by the same name) for me, she captures the essence of a "Yes!" life.

It's the story of a wealthy, orphaned boy, who is left, during a cocktail party, on the gold chaise-lounge of his Auntie Mame, in 1928. The wacky adventures of this pair extend from a plunge into the Deep South, to a short lived sales career, to a stint on the stage; all the while shattering conventional thinking with laborious laughter.

Auntie Mame led an opulent, flamboyant, exuberant and infectious lifestyle; she inspired intrigue, captured my imagination and encouraged me to be curious. The world was her playground and she believed that life was too short to live in dabbles of limited proportions.

When the stock market crashed a year later so did her world but not her resourcefulness for life. No more extravagant parties or nights on the town, she couldn't pay her servants and now she was responsible for the care and upbringing of Patrick, her ward. She was not derailed for long, however. She did what other people did in those times—she picked herself up, brushed herself off and looked for work.

211

She hadn't worked a day in her life yet somehow she found the courage and strength to let go of her former lifestyle; beginning an amusing, short lived career selling toys at Macy's Department Store.

Everyone has an Auntie Mame in their life, someone who sparks imagination, illuminates possibilities and proves to us how much joy and fun the world can be. These people touch our soul or true self and inadvertently bring us closer to God.

Sally the Tramp first sparked my imagination, at the age of ten. Astride a chocolate mare she journeyed on to my parent's ranch near the Sacramento River one day. Like a character out of the Wild West everything she owned was tied to her saddle bags. Her tattered felt hat shadowed her well worn features and her long over-coat barely hid the pistol she had holstered at her hip. Our family gathered round the dinner table as Sally spun amusing tales of her adventurous life under the stars with only a bed roll, frying pan and a change of clothes. The next day she rode off as she had come. But I was changed. I had had a glimpse of the world beyond the ranch; I'd glimpsed a free-spirited woman with an extraordinary sense of humor whose ability to adapt to her surroundings was admirable. I didn't want to be her; I just wanted to emulate her spirit.

Think back. Reflect for a moment on the people you've met who've taken the road less traveled and reached beyond the status quo; someone who sparked your Spirit causing you to think differently about the world. Maybe you had an Auntie Mame figure like my Aunt Daisy who in 1945 was the gossip of Red Bluff, California when she sported a bikini, smoked cigars just for the fun of it. These people with their sense of humor have turned life on its very pointed head, shown us another view of life and given us the greatest gift of all, curiosity. These people are the essence of a healer.

We usually envision a healer as someone in flowing white who lays their hand on you and Ka-pow! Ka-zam! Bam! You are healed. I don't for a moment believe that this is how to recognize a healer.

212

Healers are everyday people who meet everyday challenges with acceptance, curiosity and transforming humor. They practice the art of acceptance, with the understanding that curiosity opens the door to your true spirit, and humor changes attitudes and perceptions.

Therefore you don't have to be a rocket scientist, religious or even intelligent to be a healthy communicator with yourself and others. All you have to be is accepting, curious and willing to say "YES!" to the lighter, funnier side of life. Each of us has within us the unique ability to spark imaginations, inspire creativity and change the world with our Spirit. We are here to Live, Live, Live and have the most fun possible.

This chapter is explicitly, unequivocally and positively dedicated to the YELLOW in all of us. Put on your party hats; whoopee cushion lovers unite; let your Yellow come out to play! Personality styles, courage, forgiveness, communication with your body, mind and Soul or Spirit are all processes I have shared with you. These processes help you connect with your inner self and thereby increase your ability to be the leader of your life and to help lead others. However, let me warn you—you've got to be crazy to say "YES!" to life. Or at least it helps. Of course I mean *crazy* in the best, most delightful, sense of the word.

Crazy to me is the "Aw, Yes!" Spirit that says why not, I'll try anything! Self-discovery can be serious stuff; especially if your life depends upon it, and it does. If you want to change your life you have to get serious about it. However, as I have explained previously, it's all about balance.

Your ability to create healthy supportive **Blue** relationships, your **Green** capacity to organize and your **Red** competency to reach goals are vital elements, but without your **Yellow** sense of humor, joy and enthusiasm for life, you are dead.

Too often people dive into self-improvement programs like a duck without feathers. They get their feet wet but wonder why they can't stay afloat. The truth is, they try too hard. Using their Blue, Green

213

and Red savvy gives them structure and determination, but if there is no joy in the doing, it all becomes wearisome and tedious. That's when great intentions fall to the side. In fact, that's what ninety percent of all diets are about: following a structured program that tells you what, when and how to eat and exercise. If you don't find some kind of delight in the process, before you can say *baklava*, you are riding a chocolate cake.

Your only saving grace is your ability to live in the moment, have a sense of joy for the small pleasures of everyday life. Your Yellow is vital to your ability to say "Yes!" to the changes you want to make in your life. Here is a list of Yellow qualities and why they will help you achieve what you want.

Yellows have no perception of time. Therefore they measure their progress by how they feel and how much fun they're having. This can be quite helpful if you are feeling discouraged, because the process of change is taking too long. "I have been trying to say "Yes!" for years. How long does it take to get to "Yes?" Answer: There is no place to get to and the evolution of change takes whatever time it takes.

Life is a practice and like golf or ballet, some things come to us easily and others take longer to learn. Have you ever noticed how fast time passes when you are having fun? Find the fun in the challenge, no matter how challenging it is. If you step back and observe the humor even in the most horrific of circumstances your balance will be restored. If you allow your body, mind and Spirit a dollop of fun, then whatever you have to work through will become much easier.

Yellows are risk-takers who will try anything at least once. When accompanied by the Blue, Green and Red sagacity or common sense, they will bring a spark of enthusiasm to whatever they attempt. Risk is not scary. It's the events and apprehension before the action that freezes us in our tracks. Once you have taken the attitude, "Oh, why not?" risk itself becomes a comfortable act. Therefore the more often you are willing to risk, the easier it is to make calm level-headed decisions.

Yellows have a highly developed intuition. Energetically they have a visceral sense of life and they use this ability to sense whether a person, place or thing is good for them or not. This is a great advantage when you want to attract a rich and rewarding life. Intuition is, so to speak, your body, mind and Spirit's radar, detecting and comprehending the nuances of the world around you.

As you heighten your reliance on your intuition, you will be able to filter out negative and harmful energies and attract the types of energies that will lead you to sustainable feelings of joy and peace.

Yellows are levity seekers. They enjoy creating joy for themselves and others. By lightening up and finding joy in the most mundane of activities, they can move any situation from sad to glad. Of course humor must always be used appropriately; however, humor is the antidote for breaking the tension and managing an awkward situation. Never underestimate the power of humor.

When it comes to freeform thinking, your Yellow trait helps you daydream. It lets you empty your mind of unwanted, unnecessary stuff. Your imagination and ability to create are generated by your sense of humor and, coincidentally, your humor is sparked by your unlimited imagination. Therefore fantasizing and thinking way, way outside the box will assist you in cultivating a warm, loving, humor-filled life. And what better way to stay healthy and stress-free!

"A sense of humor implies a confident person… If you can joke about a tough situation, you're saying, 'Yes, it's serious, but I'm in control."
Anonymous

The Health Benefits of Humor And Laughter

Laughter activates the chemistry of the will to live and increases our capacity to fight disease. Laughing relaxes the body and reduces problems associated with high blood pressure, strokes, arthritis, and ulcers. Tickling your funny bone also seems to cause the body to release natural painkillers, increasing our tolerance for discomfort. It also mobilizes infection-fighting antibodies, such as immunoglobulin found in the saliva. Other research suggests that a sense of humor decreases blood levels of stress hormones, such as adrenaline and cortisol, which make us vulnerable to illness.

A good hearty laugh can help:

- reduce stress
- lower blood pressure
- elevate mood
- boost immune system
- improve brain function

- protect the heart
- connect you to others
- foster instant relaxation
- make you feel good

"Doctor I have a ringing in my ears."
"Don't answer!"

Henny Youngman

More Good News!

According to the latest research laughing is like an aerobic workout. Since I'm always looking for a way out of exercising, this is very good news!

"People are surprised to learn that laughter is actually a form of exercise," says William Fry M.D., associate clinical professor emeritus of psychiatry at Stanford University. According to Dr. Fry, laughing 100 times as day gives the same boost to your heart and lungs as 10 minutes of rowing.

Five Good Reasons to Use Humor:

✻ Humor is contagious.

✻ Humor helps people to connect.

✻ Humor defuses difficult situations.

✻ Humor is a managing device.

✻ Happy people are healthier and tend to live longer.

Test Your "Yes" Sense of Humor

Here is a short questionnaire to assess your sense of humor and to remind you, *Don't Sweat the Small Stuff* as Richard Carlson, Ph.D. says in his book of the same title.

1. At the dinner party a favorite serving platter with a luscious roast on it smashes to the floor. You...

- Explain to your guests that your recent crash course in meal preparation has been a success.

- Cry, then blame your dog for tripping you.

- Wipe down the roast and worry about the platter later.

2. Your dog mistakes one of your new high-heels for a rawhide chew toy. You...

- Bronze it as a testament to man's best friend.

- Toss him the other one and let him "go to town."

- Find a new place to store your shoes from now on.

3. At an executive dinner you make a grand entrance with toilet paper trailing from your heel. You...

- Flee red-faced from the scene.

- Drape it over your shoulder like a shawl.

- Stuff it in your clothing for extra padding.

4. Each day during rush-hour traffic, your inclination is to…

- Jive to Aretha Franklin's "*Respect*" so your fellow commuters can hear.

- Listen to books on tape.

- Grit your teeth, wish you had an armored tank so you could run over the lot of them.

5. You work hard on a project for the boss. He calls you "a good little helper." Your response…

- Why thanks. I think you're a good little dictator too.

- I'm more of a doer than a helper.

- Jokingly you offer to wash his car next week.

So how was that for you? Of course there is no right or wrong answers here. Yet it does give you some alternative actions. Only you know what the appropriate response would be in any given situation. However I favor the most outrageous responses myself.

"Don't get your knickers in a not. Nothing is solved and it just makes you walk funny."
Kathryn Carpenter

There is no doubt that humor can alter your perceptions and change your life. Some research suggests that laughter may also reduce the risk of heart disease. Historically, research has shown that distressing emotions (depression, anger, anxiety, and stress) are all related to heart disease. A study done at the University of Maryland Medical Center suggests that a good sense of humor and the ability to laugh at stressful situations helps mitigate the damaging physical effects of distressing emotions.

Expand Your Sense of Humor

The sound of roaring laughter is far more contagious than any cough, sniffle, or sneeze. Humor and laughter can cause a domino effect of joy and amusement, as well as setting off a number of positive physical effects. Using laughter to lighten your Spirits and health is the best form of preventive medicine. Here are fifteen ways to expand your sense of humor and laughter.

Collect Humor

Make a humor portfolio. Collect humorous photos of people, animals, signs or newspaper headlines. Whatever makes you laugh is what *you* want in your collection.

Listen to what makes you laugh. If Moe, Larry and Curly of the Three Stooges ring your bell, go for it. If George Carlin, George Lopez or George Bush make you laugh, add them to your collection. Collect humorous CDs and listen to them often. Stash a few comedic CDs in your car for the rush hour commute.

Assemble a library of comic relief. Every day, make a practice of reading a fun book, magazine etc. I recommend you read something funny before you read the newspaper, so you'll be able to see the lighter side of what's being reported.

Put together a compilation of DVD's for a rainy day. When you are feeling down physically or emotionally grab your tissues and put in an old black and white comedy and force yourself to laugh until you have tears. This will cure your ails.

Fung Shui for Humor. Designate a corner to home for your humor collection. Posters, CDs, DVDs, books, magazines, statuettes, figurines or what have you. This will lighten the energy of a room. When you need a lift, just crawl into your corner and smile.

Waiting for Humor. The next time you are at the dentist or doctor, or waiting for tickets to a movie, strike up a conversation with those next to you. Start by asking them about their day or what they do, and then ask, "Have you ever had anything funny happen? Listen and enjoy the moment, then later make a note.

Willingly look foolish. When you make mistakes, have egg on your face, trail through life with toilet paper or dress up when you should have dressed down, get over it. Be willing to laugh at yourself. Write down the experience so you can laugh harder at your next faux-pas.

Body Humor

Your body needs your brand of humor. Take time to try these exercises, to relieve stress and bring balance back to your body and mind:

Cross your legs twice. Wrap your legs around each other twice if you can. Tell people you are now a human cork screw. By the way, this is a great yoga move to stretch your hip muscles.

Scrunch up your face to your nose as tight as you can. It will relax your facial muscles and change your mood. Do this in the elevator and you'll create quite a stir.

Push your belly way out as if you are pregnant. Then draw it in real tight. Do this over and over again, as you waddle around like a duck. This will loosen your abdomen, where you hold your tension, and of course it'll raise eyebrows.

Go from chuckles to guffaws. For no apparent reason, work your body up from a muffled chuckle, to a pleasant laugh and then to a gut wrenching belly laugh that has you on your knees, wheezing.

Make boat sounds. Press your lips together and make the sound of a motor boat revving up for a race. Start slowly, then step on the throttle and shift to high gear. Watch out for the wake that follows. Everyone will either think you're crazy or they'll join you. Who cares— either way you are having fun.

Twist into a funny shape. What humorous body positions can you make up?

Mind Humor

In this age of high tech, high speed, and high content, it is no wonder our minds get weary by the end of the day. We find ourselves watching the boob tube to unwind, which really doesn't work because all we are doing is loading up on junk-food-TV. Here are a few exercises to help you lighten up your mind and refresh your Spirit.

Create or purchase joke affirmation cards and place them in a fish bowl (no fish). Take one out everyday before work. Read it, carry it with you and refer to it during the day.

Be curious about how life works. Your childlike curiosity is the springboard to accepting yourself and the world lightly. Curiosity is an inquiry into wonder and awe.

Doodle in the sand or sandbox. Doodling is a lost art that needs you to revive it. Meditation sandboxes with a rake, child size sandboxes and the entire shoreline of any ocean are waiting for you to empty your mind and doodle.

Exercise your convertible mind. Use your talent for serendipity to convert what others consider accidents or misfortunes into something useful. Absorb new, unexpected or even unpleasant experiences and be changed by them. At the same time, be proactive in your thinking so you can take appropriate action. Yes, turn lemons into lemonade.

Be a sponge for the light side. Everything has a lighter side if you are willing to rest your mind and look for ways to lighten up. Your mind will thank you and so will the people in your life.

Soul Humor

Your soul is a neutral space that never cries or laughs. But because it is so connected to the body and mind, laughter is always good for the soul. Here are a few ideas to lighten up your Spirit and feed your soul:

Celebrate every holiday that you possibly can. Think of it—Ground Hog's Day could give you the giggles. Simply set the table with a bowl of dirt (ground Oreo Cookies), carefully spear chocolate fortune cookies and plant them in the bowl. Let everyone dig for their fortune. Supply sunglasses in case there is a glare from the February sun.

Visit every sunset and sunrise with a sense of awe. Let your soul be touched by colors, stillness, appreciation and wonder of a day past and a day anew. Raise your arms to the sky and give praise.

Submerge yourself in Mother Earth; smell it, taste it, sit on it. Become aware of the earth's energy by planting a few plants, pulling a few weeds. Gardening is a great way to center yourself —and so is mud wrestling.

Get crafty with your bare hands. There is nothing like hand-made gifts from one's soul to another. Lots of people, movie stars to scientists, race car drivers to nerds, are crafty. Take up knitting or crochet and make simple scarves and hats for the homeless. Your soul will thank you.

Breathe in the organics of life. Your nose is the snifter to your soul. That is why the smell of fresh baked bread can send you reeling. Your sense of smell travels to your brain at an alarming speed. Try these smells: fresh cut wood, fresh cut flowers, moist dirt, or salty sea air. What smells do you love?

Using Humor to Lighten-up

There are many situations in daily life that beg for the lighter side. Sometimes you just have to stir up the Universe with your craziness or silliness. For instance, a friend of mine, who is a personal coach, confessed to leading a coaching group (in certification) topless. Guess I ought to mention it was a conference call! She told them she was showing up as her authentic, playful self with no hidden agenda and then she invited them to join her.

There are other ways to lighten up stale situations. For instance, there are the ole lighten-up standards such as meeting your hubby at the door wrapped in saran wrap and letting him unwrap the surprise, or picking him up from work wearing a long coat with nothing under it. You might add a little spice by strutting around in a bathing suit and high-heels and posing as a Betty Gable pin-up girl or just for the hell of it serving your friends cocktails in a French maid's outfit. I may have dialed into the naked channel, but you get the picture.

"By the time a child reaches nursery school, he or she will laugh about 300 times a day. Adults laugh an average of 17 times a day."
"Science of Laughter" Discovery Health

The things you really want to watch out for are the *downers*. These are the people who, when you say *blue*, say *black*, or you wish them, "Good day!" and their comeback is, "What for?" These are what I consider problematic people. Sprinkled everywhere in your life are people who are oblivious to their behavior and unaware that there's a problem. You work with or for them, you live with them, love them or are related to them. Which means you cannot easily detach yourself from them.

Even worse, *they* could be *you*! Of course, you'd want to know it, so let me introduce a gallery of everyday downers, with antidotes you can use to lighten up your view.

Meet The Downers—And Their Antidotes

The Downer: *Nanna Yabut*

Oh, so you think that's a good idea? "Yabut I don't want to be a
wet blanket," Nanna Yabut says, "I tried that once and well frankly, it
didn't work. You think I oughta try a healthy diet? Yabut it's too hard
and I'm too fat. I've been told my arthritis keeps acting up because I
don't want to change direction or move easily. Yabut I don't understand
why I got passed over for the promotion, I'm so positive and such a
hard worker. Yabut the boss just doesn't get me." Nanna Yabut is just
making an ass of herself.

"Laughter is very powerful medicine.
It can lower stress, dissolve anger and unite families
in their resolve to overcome troubled times."

Nanna's Antidote: *"Yes!" I Can*

This is the magic antidote that will banish Nanna Yabut from your life forever. Think this way:

"I am a can-do person! Oh I know my limits—God knows, everyone in the world lets me know my limits. However there is nothing canned about my God-given potential and ability to try new things, even if I fail. Besides, life shrinks or expands in proportion to one's courage, and failure is just a promising stepping stone toward success. I move easily and freely through life, enjoying every moment. I keep a "God Can" at my desk to hold my dreams and aspirations because I say "Yes!" to life and I can do it."

The Downer: *Waukeen Wounded*

"Boy, oh boy, do I have a headache! It's like a piercing feeling. My boss is a jerk, the traffic stinks and the cops are out to get me. Everyone is out to get me. When I am driving my car, there they are. My idea of defensive driving is strapping a machine gun on the front of my SUV. I haven't spoken to my brother for years. Why? I don't know. I get so angry, I hold grudges. I could be someone who makes a difference in the world, if I could just get rid of the pain. Who wants to bother with that self-help mumbo jumbo?"

"There is way too much fear in the world today, life was never meant to be taken so seriously."

Dr. Cathryn Morter, N.D., D.C., C.H.

Waukeen's Antidote: *Ima Well Healed*

Okay, Waukeen, it's time to change your name and switch to this way of thinking:

"I have a well healed life! I've discovered the fountain of unlimited wealth. It doesn't take hard work, there is no sugar daddy, and it's not even illegal. The Fountain spews abundance to me when I am giving and forgiving. It's so simple: the more I give to others, the less time I have to be angry or frustrated. The act of forgiving is a way of paying myself forward. When I for-give others and myself for past transgressions, it's like putting money in the bank. Prosperity, opulence, riches beyond my wildest imagination is transformed into priceless peace of mind."

The Downer: *Gracie Gossip*

"I was sitting in the doctor's office the other day, just listening. That's when I overheard about a new disease. It starts in your big toe and, oh my gawd, after some aggravation it spreads up the right leg, through the hip and settles in the left pinky. Oh it's so bad, really bad. It's called Pinkenitis. There's a new drug on the market that is supposed to help. It will eat your liver, but your pinky won't fall off." There is nothing like a good drama. It's the trauma drama of life that makes the world go around. Oh it doesn't have to be true or good for you. It's all about drama, baby.

"Without humor one's thought processes are likely to become stuck and narrowly focused, leading to increased distress."
Association for Applied and Therapeutic Humor

Gracie's Antidote: *Napoleon I Scream*

"Okay, now, in order to take charge of your life, you have to become a little Napoleonic. As the leader of your life, it is your responsibility for the safety and well being of the troops. Your troops—body, mind and Spirit—are depending on you to keep them healthy."

Who are you listening to, spending your precious time with and wasting your valuable energy on? Let go of the storms of trauma and drama, and feather your cap with the right choices.

The Downer: *Cleo, Queen of Denial*

"I don't see it, so it's not there. If I turn sideways, I will never see it. Maybe it will just go away on its own. Denial is not a river and I am not going to take the plunge. Why is my blood pressure skyrocketing? Could it be that I am not willing to face a long-standing problem and solve it? Everything is okay, I get by, I don't have to be happy, I just get by. I am of the philosophy that if I never start anything, I won't get hurt and I won't have to end anything. I'll stay on my barge with my rose colored glasses and try not to make an asp of myself."

"Without humor one's thought processes are likely to become stuck and narrowly focused leading to increased distress."

Association for Applied and Therapeutic Humor

Cleo's Antidote: *Les Face It*

"Turn yourself around. Right here... Right here in front of you is the answer to moving forward. Stop leading a mediocre existence when you can be living fully in the world of reality. *Face it*—you have a beautiful future. *Face it*—you can be what you want to be. *Face it*— you can do it. Some things are going to hurt you, disappoint you and distress you. Bite the bullet, take the bull by the horns and plunge into the unknown. *Face it*—you are talented, charming, beautiful, handsome, witty and intelligent, so stop settling for less than you deserve."

Writing Down the Stories of Life

There are three reasons for you to write down everyday funny stories.

✿ Writing things down helps you recall them more vividly later.

✿ You will remember and appreciate just how wonderful it is to be human in a human body.

✿ On those down days, you will be uplifted by reading your humor journal.

An Excerpt from My Own Humor Journal:

Oreo is No Cookie

Our family was in the kitchen preparing Thanksgiving dinner. Every year is different; we choose a country to be thankful for and this year it was Greece. So the kitchen was filled with olive oil, stuffed grape leaves and rack of lamb. I dashed to the store for baklava and upon opening the door Naomi (my granddaughter) exclaimed, "We can't find Oreo." Oreo is no cookie he is Naomi's pet hamster. She loves this little rodent, I figure someone has to.

Anyway, here is the scene. Wensdai, Naomi, Ivory and their Aunt Susan are on the floor calling "Oreo!" Ron, their father, straddled the top of the kitchen counter declaring he'd found the little black and white ball of fur. Oreo had chewed his way out of his cage, skittered up the cabinet and slipped into a narrow gap between. The only reason he was detected at all was the fine sawdust drifting in the air below. The funny thing is, we could have let Oreo continue to chew his way out. but instead, after some poking and prodding, Ron, the Tool Man, found a drill and bored a hole in the bottom of the cabinet and freed the little bugger.

We laughed for hours afterwards. Thanksgiving is a time to be thankful and this year our family was cooking, eating and laughing together. I was thankful for our Greek dinner, thankful for Greece and thankful that Oreo was still in his cage.

Humor is not necessarily something that comes from external sources. It is germinated from deep within your soul. It's what makes the rest of you tick and tick well. Take time to discover, listen and cherish the humorous happenings of your life.

"When we laugh, natural killer cells, which destroy tumors and viruses, increase, along with Gamma-interferon (a disease-fighting protein), T-cells (important for our immune system) and B-cells (which make disease-fighting antibodies). As well as lowering blood pressure, laughter increases oxygen in the blood, which also encourages healing."
"Science of Laughter" Discovery Health Website

Resource Center

👥 *When You Look Like Your Passport Photo, It's Time to Go Home*, by Erma Bombeck, is all about laughing at yourself and the human condition. Any of Erma's books is worth a chuckle. My favorite quote: "*The continental breakfast is not designed to make you thin. Even if it is eaten in small pieces, it will expand and distribute itself on your hips and thighs until you are molded into its image.*"

👥 One of my favorite films is **Patch Adams**, based on the book, **Gesundheit: Good Health is a Laughing Matter.** Robin Williams portrays Hunter D. "Patch" Adams founder of a hospital in the wilderness area of West Virginia—a hospital without patients. There were only two staff members who, like Patch Adams, believed in the healing power of humor and compassion.

Ki Exercise # 11

In this moment, breathe into your abdomen and breathe out. Expand your lungs and fill your body with new life. Find a comfortable place to be alone in the silence. Begin tapping your head gently with your fingers, starting from the back of the head and moving forward. Tap the top of your head and the sides. Work your way around to your forehead, nose, eyes, cheeks and chin. Let the vibration soothe you and calm you.

Close your eyes and bring to mind something you are grateful for, then smile at its magnificence. Notice how your body feels when you smile. Breathe in. Breathe out. Raise your arms above your head, in praise to the Universal God that supports you and loves you. Spread your arms as if they were wings and stretch your body in willingness to change. Wrap your arms around your body and embrace change.

Bring to mind something you found humor in today. Smile and enjoy reliving the moment in your mind. Notice how your body feels when you smile. Breathe in. Breathe out. Straighten your spine and stretch your body to touch your toes. It's okay if you can't reach, it's the stretch that counts. Touch mother earth with your finger tips and direct your energy to the earth. It needs your love.

Breathe in and breathe out. You are blessed with the power to change your life. Appreciate what you have, change will come naturally. Stretch your entire body from head to toe. As you stretch your body, you open your mind and as you open your mind, your soul will sing. Relax and open your eyes and stay in the calm of the moment to reflect and heal your life.

Chapter 12

The Dream Seekers

*"Truth needs heroes. You have only one heart and it is a single seat.
It is not a musical chair. Be loyal to your heart."*

Sai Baba

The Power of Dreams

Dreams are powerful. Studies show that dreaming gives the brain time to recoup and refresh, as well as time to process everyday experiences. Filled with a myriad of symbols, dreams can tell us a great deal about ourselves and how we perceive life. As an illustration, I'd like to share with you a dream of mine, one that changed the course of my life.

One Night When I Was Sleeping...

I had a dream that I was sitting around a campfire with my family, half-listening to the stories we'd all heard so many times before. As my mind drifted, I saw, through the flames of the campfire, a golden light glimmering in the distance, across an expanse of water.

I was somehow drawn to this light, and I told the family that I wanted to find its source. Yet the only person I could talk into going with me—albeit reluctantly—was my husband. We boarded a boat to cross the water, and the two of us stood on deck, watching our families wave good-bye.

We were halfway across when my husband decided he didn't want to go. He jumped into the water, pulling me with him. That's when I discovered I was shackled to him at the ankle. Deep into the water we plunged, struggling. He pulled me back toward the shore we had left, wanting to go where things were comfortable. But somehow I knew I couldn't do that. I reached down to my ankle and, at the touch of my hand, the shackle fell away.

A tinge of sadness came over me, as I watched him swim away. Then I began what seemed like a long, arduous swim for my life. Exhausted, lungs burning, I kept swimming toward the light. After awhile I blacked out, and when I came to, I found myself lying on a rocky shore. There, off in the distance, was the golden light I yearned to see. Brushing myself off, I walked away from the shore and up over the hill into my new life.

Reaching A Defining Moment

The significance of this dream is that it represents a defining moment when a decision was made to move toward what is paramount in life. It symbolized the reality I had finally recognized: that if I wanted to change my life and live a life of loving service, I had to let go of antiquated beliefs of my past. I had to be willing to swim through the watery test of the unknown to experience the golden light of God-Spirit.

The golden light is there for all of us. It is over the next hill, around the bend and mostly assuredly it is in your heart. There is no place to go to get the light. The light is within you, you are the light.

There is only one Spirit in and through all things there is only one purpose for all human kind.

By expressing your true self, and being a healthy communicator, you are holding the golden light of love to make clear the way for others. What are you here for? The answer is the same for all of us: our only purpose is to hold the light.

You Can Make The Ultimate Difference

Perfection consists not in doing extraordinary things, but in doing ordinary things extraordinarily well. Neglect nothing; the most trivial action may be performed to God."

Angelique Arnauld

You have been asleep for many years or lifetimes; it is time to become consciously aware. If all the years between birth and death are frittered away in seeking food, shelter, comfort, security and pleasures, as animals do, humankind is then condemned to a further life-sentence of misery, pain and war. It is time to end this antiquated paradigm. It is time to give 100% of our energy, individually and collectively, to building a new type of world, a world of peace.

World peace is not some far-off fallacy that only gurus on mountain tops preach about. World peace can be—and I believe *will* be—accomplished through the art of giving. Saying "Yes!" to life presents new meaning to the word giving. Giving is the act of seeking opportunities and relationships for the purpose of making the world a better place, one person, one company or one country at a time. I know that sounds like some virtuously composed car commercial, but it is the truth.

The Smallest of Gifts Can Make A Difference

A soul-based life, a "Yes!" life, is a life of giving, lovingly and un-conditionally, without questions or answers, and with the sole purpose of making a difference. Remember, even the smallest of gifts can make a difference. You are here on this earth with a purpose. Are you still searching for your purpose? Are you still wondering how you can make a difference in the world? Discover your purpose through the act of giving. You will, through your generosity, increase the cycle of giving and receiving and help bring about world peace.

If you find that life is flat,
Full of this, with none of that,
Try giving!
Introspection makes it flatter;
A few more years—what will it matter?
Try giving!
If the world is dark and bitter;
Things all tend to make a quitter—
Try giving!
Forget yourself in helping others;
Know that all men are your brothers,
You will see then life is sweeter
Than you thought, and far completer—
When you give!

Margaret Gordon Kuhlman

The Dream Seekers

There are dream seekers among us, people who seek answers to unanswerable questions, whose curiosity compels them to wander over a hill, around the next bend or look deeply inside themselves. Their curiosity and willingness to explore inspires us; we emulate and admire their tenacity and dedication.

However, the page has turned. When you said "Yes!" to life, you officially became a Dream Seeker. You are free to live a vital life with an eagerness to learn and a willingness to change. Your insatiable thirst to question, create and produce will lead you to express your true self like you never have before.

It has been the intention of this book to open your mind and to guide you deeper into the world of personal exploration and discovery. My personal intention is to give you experimentation tools for a "Yes!" life. Much as a child would with a chemistry set or a carton of Lego® blocks, I want you to ask yourself, "What things will I stir up? Where will I build it? How will I make a difference in the world?"

Fasten your divine seat belt, because from now on you are on the ride of your life. And, as Betty Davis once said, "…it's going to be a bumpy ride!"

As you practice the exercises and suggestions from the previous chapters, you will notice both subtle and drastic changes that are signs a shift is occurring. Don't let this deter you. You have made a decision to take charge of who, what, where and how your life progresses. You will stub your toe or fall flat on your face. You will falter, lose confidence and gain it back. You will have challenges and changes that will test your purpose. However, when you said "Yes!" to *your* life, you said "Yes!" to the Spirit within you, the most potent energy in the universe, and that alone will be enough to support you.

When you said "YES!" to life, you gave up the right to be like everyone else. That is why you draw experiences to yourself that will cleanse you of that which does not fit your true self. You will have these experiences over and over again, until you see that the past no longer works. Let go of the past. Stop trying to get from others what you think you missed in childhood, marriage or other circumstances. You will never find anyone who is enough, except the God self, the true self within you.

Only when you give up totally and are consumed by the golden light of love will you truly live a life of blissful peace. Now is the time!

"There are people who put their dreams in a little box and say,
'Yes, I've got dreams, of course I've got dreams.'
Then they put the box away and bring it out once in awhile
to look in it and, yep, they're still there.
These are great dreams, but they never even get out of the box.
It takes an uncommon amount of guts to put your dreams
on the line, to hold them up and say, "How good or bad am I?
That's where courage comes in."

Erma Bombeck

Universal Spirit is always there for you; it will never give up on you. It is your soul's connection that is pleading and begging for you to open up, express your true self, and lead a more loving and caring existence. It is asking you to take your dreams out of the box and put them on the line. What is your dream, what is your soul's desire?

Isn't it time you said, "Yes!" to Life?

Words to Change Your Life

Words are vibrations of energy. Whatever you say or do vibrates and resounds in the heart of you and everyone it touches. Here are a few words for you to spend time with. Read slowly, and let your mind wash over the words. Then wrap your mind around the affirmation that follows. Make a copy of your favorites and put them up where you can recall them during the day.

> I took a piece of plastic clay
> And idly fashioned it one day,
> And as my fingers pressed it, still
> It moved and yielded to my will.
>
> I came again when days were past;
> The bit of clay was hard at last,
> The form I gave it still it bore,
> But I could change the form no more!
>
> I took a piece of living clay,
> And gently pressed it day by day,
> And molded with my power and art
> A young child's soft and yielding heart.
>
> Anonymous

Affirmation:

I am the artist of my life. I co-create my life. With guidance from within I create the kind of life that feeds my soul and the souls of the people who I meet. I am grateful. Thank you, God.

❀ ❀ ❀

The Road Not Taken

Two roads diverged in a yellow wood,
And sorry I could not travel both
And be one traveler, long I stood
And looked down one as far as I could
To where it bent in the undergrowth;
  Then took the other, as just as fair,
  And having perhaps the better claim,
  Because it was grassy and wanted wear;
Though as for that the passing there
Had worn them really about the same,
And both that morning equally lay
In leaves no step had trodden black.

Oh, I kept the first for another day!
Yet knowing how way leads on to way,
I doubted if I should ever come back.

  I shall be telling this with a sigh
  Somewhere ages and ages hence:
Two roads diverged in a wood, and I—
I took the one less traveled by,
And that has made all the difference.

Robert Frost

Affirmation:

I open my heart to the sound of my soul. I daringly go where my heart leads me. I now choose to grow closer to God through my words and actions. Today I am thankful for my life.

Music is like a soft breeze blowing by.
Music is like the clear blue sky.
Music is a beautiful sound made by people,
It is the sound when spring comes and goes.
Music is the night when it's bright,
It's the sun when it shines.
Music is my light.

Patsy Diaz

Affirmation:

Thank you, God, for the golden light of love shining within all people, places and things; I now use this light to make a difference in the world with love. I now let my heart sing the music it is meant to sing.

❁ ❁ ❁

Ah, snug lie those that slumber
Beneath Conviction's roof.
Their floors are sturdy lumber,
Their windows weatherproof.
But I sleep cold forever
And cold sleep all my kind,
For I was born to shiver
In the draft from an open mind.

Phyllis McGinley

Affirmation:

Thank you, God, for a curious mind and a willingness to be uncomfortable as I grow my true self. I now express my authentic true self in everything I do, for I know who walks with me.

243

Ship Across the Sky

White wings across the morning,
Dark sails against the moon,
Scudding along in the spindrift
While the trade-winds croon;

Dark hull against the blue,
White spars across the sky—
Like a song from out of the distance
And clear as a sea-gull's cry;

Hull down against the horizon
And royals across the gray,
I saw it fade into the distance
Sailing my dreams away.

Louis L'Amour

Affirmation

Today is the day I walk with my dreams. Whatever I do today I will take one small step toward my dream. I now open to all possibilities; I expand my confidence as I try new things and risk for change.

✿ ✿ ✿

The million little things that drop into your hands
The small opportunities each day brings
He leaves us free to use or abuse
And goes unchanging along His silent way.

Helen Keller

Affirmation:

Thank you, God, for all that you have given me. Even the smallest of tasks I will do with enthusiastic joy. I am blessed with opportunity, talent and peace of mind. Thank you, God.

There's not a cliff too awesome
nor a stream too swift or deep,
nor a haunted hill too eerie,
nor a mountain trail too steep
for the questing heart to venture
or the eager breath to dare.

Lorraine Usher Babbitt

Affirmation:

My true self knows where I shall venture to what I shall do to give of myself so that I can grow closer to the one source of all things. I am a daring person. I will try anything because I know that Spirit is always there to support me.

※ ※ ※

Laugh and the world laughs with you,
Weep and you weep alone;
For the sad old earth must borrow its mirth,
But has trouble enough of its own.

Sing and the hills will answer,
Sigh and it's lost on the air;
For the echoes bound to a joyful sound,
But shrink from voicing a care.

Ella Wheeler Wilcox

Affirmation:

Thank you, God, for the joy of this moment. In this moment I am filled with love for all human kind. I am an instrument of peace. I now commit to enjoying the love and excitement of each moment.

245

I Wandered Lonely As A Cloud

I wandered lonely as a cloud
That floats on high o'er vales and hills,
When all at once I saw a crowd,
A host, of golden daffodils;
Beside the lake, beneath the trees,
Fluttering and dancing in the breeze.

Continuous as the stars that shine
And twinkle on the milky way,
They stretched in never-ending line
Along the margin of a bay:
Ten thousand saw I at a glance,
Tossing their heads in sprightly dance.

The waves beside them danced, but they
Out-did the sparkling leaves in glee;
A poet could not be but gay,
In such a jocund company!
I gazed—and gazed—but little thought
What wealth the show to me had brought:

For oft, when on my couch I lie
In vacant or in pensive mood,
They flash upon that inward eye
Which is the bliss of solitude;
And then my heart with pleasure fills,
And dances with the daffodils.

William Wordsworth

Affirmation:

My heart is full of life. Everywhere I turn is the energy of Spirit.
I open my mind and soul to all that I see. Thank you, God, for the
love and guidance through the dance of life.

My Shadow

I have a little shadow that goes in and out with me,
And what can be the use of him is more than I can see.
He is very, very like me from the heels up to the head:
And I see him jump before me, when I jump into my bed.

The funniest thing about him is the way he likes to grow
Not at all like proper children, which is always very slow;
For he sometimes shoots up taller, like an Indian-rubber-ball,
And he sometimes gets so little that there's none of him at all.

He hasn't got a notion of how children ought to play,
And can only make a fool of me in every sort of way.
He stays so close beside me, he's a coward you can see;
I'd think shame to stick to nurse as that shadow sticks to me!

One morning, very early, before the sun was up,
I rose and found the shining dew on every buttercup;
But my lazy little shadow, like an arrant sleepy-head,
Had stayed at home behind me and was fast asleep in bed.

Robert Louis Stevenson

Affirmation:

Everywhere I go there I am. I cannot hide from myself. I now stand up for who I am and what I am. I am here to stand up for the truth. I am here to hold the light of love to show the way for myself and others to express the true self. Thank you, God.

꧁ ꧁ ꧁

When doubts and fears are growing,
  It's hard to keep on going
    From day to day not knowing
      Just what the end will be.
Take each day as you find it,
  For each day leaves behind it
    A chance to start anew.

Gertrude Ellgas

Affirmation:

Today is the first day of my new life. I welcome all experiences that come to me because I know that each experience teaches me more about myself and my deepening relationship to the One Spirit of all things.

🕸 🕸 🕸

You can control a mad elephant;
You can shut the mouth of the bear and the tiger;
You can ride the lion;
You can play with the cobra;
By alchemy you can eke out your livelihood;
You can wander through the universe incognito
You can make vassals of the gods;
You can be ever youthful;
You can walk on water and live in fire;
But control of the mind is better and more difficult.

Thayumanavar, Indian master

Affirmation:

Thank you, God, for your guidance and love as I move through the challenges and changes of my life. I am rich beyond my wildest dreams. I take care of myself body, mind and soul. Each step is a blessing of life.

Be a Dreamer

Dare to dream
for dreamers see tomorrow.
Dare to make a wish,
for whishing makes way for hope,
and hope is what keeps us alive.

Dare to reach out
for the things no one else can see.
Be unafraid to see what
what others cannot.

Believe in your heart
and in you own goodness,
for in doing so
others will believe in them, too.

Believe in magic,
because life is full of it.

But most of all,
believe in yourself...
because within you lies
 all the magic,
the hope, the love,
and the dreams of tomorrow.

Ron Cristian

Affirmation:

Within me is the Spirit of all things. I choose to love, to dream, to experience the magic of life. In this moment I explore my dreams and aspirations. I ask myself, I wonder if? Thank you, God, for all that I am and all that I am becoming.

Bibliography

Kay Allenbaugh, *Chocolate for a Woman's Soul*, Fireside, Simon and Schuster, New York, New York, 1997.

Maya Angelou, *The Heart of a Woman*, Random House, New York, New York, 1981.

Rudolph M, Ballentine M.D., *Radical Healing*, Harmony Books, New York, New York 1999.

Herbert Benson, M.D., *Timeless Healing: The Power and Biology of Belief*, Scribner, New York, New York, 1996.

Joan Borysenko, Ph.D. *Minding the Body, Mending the Mind*, Bantam Books, New York, New York, 1988.

Sharon Anthony Bower, Gordon H. Bower, *Asserting Yourself*, Addison Wesley Publishing Company, New York, New York, 1991.

John Bradshaw, *Creating Love: The Next Great Stage of Growth*, Bantam Book, New York, New York, 1992.

Dale Carnegie, *How to Win Friends and Influence People*, Simon and Schuster, New York, New York, 1964.

Deepak Chopra, *Quantum Healing: Exploring the Frontiers of Mind/Body Medicine*, Bantam Books, New York, New York, 1990.

Deepak Chopra, *The Seven Spiritual Laws of Success*, Amber-Allen Publishing, San Rafael, California, 1994.

Stephen R. Covey, *The Seven Habits of Highly Effective People*, Simon and Schuster, New York, NewYork, 1990.

Patrick Dennis, *Auntie Mame: An Irreverent Escapade*, Vanguard Press, Inc., New York, New York, 1955.

Henry Dreher, *The Immune Power Personality*, Plume, Penguin Group, New York, NewYork, 1996.

Elrod, Juliana, and Sophia Blawyn and Suzanne Jones, *Chakra Workout*, Llewellyn Worldwide, St Paul, Minnesota, 1996.

Laura Berman Fortgang, *Living Your Best Life*, Penguin Putman Inc., New York, New York, 2001.

Richard Gerber, MD, *Vibrational Medicine*, Bear and Company Press, Rochester, Vermont, 2001.

Amit Goswami, Ph.D., *The Self-Aware Universe: How Consciousness Creates the Material World*, Penguin Putman, New York, New York, 1993.

Thomas A. Harris, M.D., *I'm OK—You're OK,* Harper & Row, Publishers, New York, New York, 1967.

Taylor Hartman, *The Color Code*, A Taylor Don Hartman Publication, Trabuco Canyon, California, 1987.

David R. Hawkins, M.D., Ph.D., *Power vs. Force,* Hay House Inc., Carlsbad California, 1995.

Louise L. Hay, *You Can Heal Your Life,* Hay House Inc., Carlsbad, California, 2004.

Napoleon Hill, *Think and Grow Rich,* Ballantine Books, New York, New York. 1937.

Ernest Holmes, Ph.D., *The Science of Mind,* Dodd, Mead and Company, New York, New York, 1938.

Louis L'Amour, *Smoke From This Alter*, Bantam Books, New York, New York, 1990.

Rob Lebow, *A Journey Into the Heroic Environment*, Prima Publishing, Rocklin, California, 1995.

Ilchi Lee, *Human Technology: A Tool Kit for Authentic Living,* Healing Society, Sedona, Arizona, 2005.

Denise Linn, *Alters: Bringing Sacred Shrines Into Your Everyday Life*, Ballantine Publishing Group, New York, New York, 1999.

A. D. K. Luk, *Law of Life,* A. D.K. Luk Publications, St. Petersburg, Florida, 1988.

Bill Moyers, *Healing and the Mind*, Double Day Publishing, New York, New York, 1993.

Howard Murphet, *Sai Baba Avatar*, Birth Day Publishing Company, San Diego, California, 1977.

M. Scott Peck, M.D., *The Road Less Traveled,* Touchstone Book, Simon and Schuster, New York, New York, 1978.

Michael Samuels, M.D., *Healing with the Minds Eye,* Summit Books, New York, New York, 1990.

Mitsugi Saotome, *Akido and the Harmony of Nature*, Shambhala Publications, Inc., Boston Massachusetts, 1986.

Anthony J. Sattilaro, M.D., *Living Well Naturally,* Houghton Mifflin Company, New York, New York, 1984.

Ronald F. Schmid, N.D., *Native Nutrition*, Healing Arts Press, Rochester, Vermont, 1994.

Al Siebert, Ph.D., *The Survivor Personality*, Practical Psychology Press, Portland, Oregon, 1993.

Bernie Siegel, M.D., Love Medicine and Miracles, Harper and Row Publishers, New York, New York, 1986.

T. Raphael Simons, *Fung Shui Step by Step*, Random House, New York, New York, 1996.

O. Carl Simonton, M.D., Stephanie Matthews-Simonton and James L. Creighton, *Getting Well Again,* Bantam Books, New York, New York, 1981.

Diane Stein, *Essential Reiki: A Complete Guide to an Ancient Healing Art,* The Crossing Press, Freedom, California, 1996.

Louise Taylor and Betty Bryant, *Ki Energy for Everybody*, Japan Publications Inc., Tokyo, and New York, 1990.

Koichi Tohei, *Kiatsu,* Ki No KenKyukai H.Q., Toyko, Japan. 1983.

Paramhansa Yogananda, *Autobiography of a Yogi*, Philosophical Library, Inc., New York, New York, 1995.

Gary Zukav, *The Seat of the Soul*, Fireside, Simon and Schuster, New York, New York, 1990.

Gary Zukav, *The Seat of the Soul*, Fireside, Simon and Schuster, New York, New York, 1990.

A Course in Miracles, Foundation for Inner Peace, Farmingdale, New York, 1983.

The Holy Bible, The American Bible Society, New York, New York, 1952.

Index

Ki Communication Programs

Every year major corporations and associations invite author Judy Pearson to present these outstanding and dynamic "Yes! Programs. Topics are available in both keynote and workshop formats. Will this be the year you say "Yes!"?

Giving "YES!" Customer Service

Leading companies are constantly reinforcing the importance of customer service. Learn how to give "Yes!" customer service creating a team work and highly productive environment.

Managing Change with "YES!" Energy

Change is the only constant in life. Learn to *A*cknowledge your unique style, *A*ccept yourself as a powerful presence and *A*ct with confidence as you manage change.

Living Life in the "YES!" Lane

Learn how to increase your influence and persuasion skills, with 10 "Yes!" Rules to Live the Optimum Life. "Love what you do, meet it with the best you have to give." Give renewed enthusiasm and passionate fire to the furnace of your dynamic organization.

The "YES!" Energy of Leadership

A true leader takes people as far as they will go, not as far as they would like them to go. Learn how to hone your "Yes!" leadership skills. Communicate with poise, strength and confidence.

To schedule a presentation, or for more information on quantity book purchases, contact:

Ki Communication
515 NW Saltzman Rd, # 749,
Portland, OR 97229,
503-520-0105
email: judyspeak@aol.com ⬥ website: www.judypearson.com

About The Author

Judy Pearson

A dynamic workshop and seminar leader, Judy Pearson is a nationally known authority on Ki Communication. Judy has been the featured speaker at hundreds of association conferences, corporate meetings, and various business groups.

She is the author of:

- **Say YES! to Life:** How to Live Life & Love It
- **Say YES! to Life Workbook**
- **Healthy Mind Healthy Body:**
  How to Use your Mind Power
  to Stay Healthy and Overcome Illness
- **Ki Up Your Life Companion**
- **The YES! to Life Journal**

Judy's clients include:

Pacificorp • Legacy Healthcare Systems •Providence Medical
Right Management Corporation • Hallmark Inns Corporation
The United States Navy
and various law firms, colleges, and universities.

Judy is the president of the Portland, Oregon-based firm of
Ki Communication, a company dedicated to
helping people make a difference in the world
by improving communications with oneself and others.